Sergei M. Eisenstein's *Potemkin*

Sergei M. Eisenstein's
POTEMKIN

A shot-by-shot presentation
by David Mayer

A DA CAPO PAPERBACK

To the three now—
Blanche, Susan, and Deborah—
and the faces in the myth long ago

Library of Congress Cataloging in Publication Data

Mayer, David.
  Sergei M. Eisenstein's Potemkin: a shot-by-shot presentation / by
David Mayer.
      p.   cm. — (A Da Capo paperback)
  Reprint. Originally published: New York: Grossman Publishers,
1972.
  ISBN 0-306-80388-7
  1. Bronenosets "Potemkin" (Motion Pictures) I. Eisenstein,
Sergei, 1898-1948. II. Title.
[PN1997.B7573M39   1990]   89-29518
791.43'72 — dc20   CIP

This Da Capo Press paperback edition of Sergei M. Eisenstein's Potemkin
is an unabridged republication of the edition published in
New York in 1972. It is reprinted by arrangement with the author.

Published by Da Capo Press, Inc.
A Subsidiary of Plenum Publishing Corporation
233 Spring Street, New York, N.Y. 10013

The print of Potemkin used in this presentation was obtained from the Museum of
Modern Art Film Department.

Frames from the film are reproduced with permission of the Rose Madell Film Library.

Acknowledgments

I knew some of the myths before I was old enough to read the subtitles. So my first acknowledgment is to my father and mother. When I was three or four they carried me at least once a week to the darkened halls where I watched the faces on the luminous gray square against the wall.

Later, when I was about seven, and old enough to perform a maneuver called "sneaking in," I often slipped unnoticed through the side door of a small neighborhood movie when the ticket collector's attention wandered. Once inside, I sat transfixed in the dark, a dweller in the myth unfolding on the screen. If I was lucky, I came in while the weekly serial was rushing to an unbelievable finish. The water was rapidly rising in the sealed room. Soon the vigorously swimming heroine would be drowned when the water reached the ceiling. How in God's name could she escape? Those of us who shared the unconscious fears stirred up so adroitly on the screen shivered a little more than the others.

At the end of the movie, just before the house lights came on, I would slip to the floor and squeeze under my curved plywood seat. There I'd hide until the usher had passed my row chanting "half tickets, half tickets." This was the signal for the ones who had paid for their tickets to hold up their stubs in proof. If you had none, you'd be asked to leave with a terse jerk of the thumb toward the exit at the rear. Sometimes, during intermission, the usher would pass down the aisle working the handle of an antiseptic spray pump to enhance the atmosphere for the next performance. When the house lights dimmed, the spray droplets would still be glistening in the air as the mercury arc lamp in the projection booth sizzled with life and the faces in the myth began to move again on the wall.

The faces still gleam in my memory. Charlie Chaplin in *Shoulder Arms* and *Easy Street,* Elmo Lincoln in the first *Tarzan of the Apes, Fantomas,* the *Golem,* Tom Mix and *Dr. Caligari.* Harry Houdini in the *Metal Monster,* and Douglas Fairbanks in *The Mark of Zorro.*

My second acknowledgment is to the 92nd Street "Y" in New York, which gave me and my friends permission to use its Kaufmann Auditorium for the 35mm. screenings of our foreign film society. Meeting each week under the self-conscious title of The Cinema Guild, we and our paying audience saw and discussed the films of men like Duvivier, Clair, Lang, Eisenstein, Hitchcock, Cocteau, and Flaherty. We were probably the first foreign film society in New York; few of us had previously seen the films we screened. We heard about them through the grapevine and would phone distributors to see if prints of these particular films were available. The film would be booked on the spot. Sometimes we'd invite a guest to discuss the film with the audience in the adjoining lounge after the showing. Often, one of us would research the film or its director as best he could and conduct the discussion himself.

The myths I was exposed to opened doors to a new world of sensibility. There were disturbing myths like *M* and *The Blue Angel.* Strangely affecting myths like *Poll de Carotte* and *The Informer.* Baffling myths like *Lot in Sodom* and *Blood of a Poet.* Astounding myths like *Storm Over Asia* and *Potemkin.* And hilarious myths like *The Italian Straw Hat* and *Le Million.*

Gradually, my interest shifted from the myth to the mythmaker; this book is a look at the clockwork in the magic. It is a pleasure to thank Miss Eileen Bowser of the Museum of Modern Art Film Department, who provided me with a complete original print of *Potemkin* for my prolonged study. Mr. James Seligmann also earns my warm thanks for his unfailing support. It is with very special gratitude that I acknowledge the perceptive contributions of my wife, Blanche, whose clear mind and skillful fingers were most helpful in preparing the manuscript.

Introduction

In 1952, the Brussels Exhibition asked film directors from many nations to nominate the ten best films in cinema history. *Potemkin* was chosen as one of the ten. Again, in 1961, *Sight and Sound,* a magazine published by the British Film Institute, asked 70 critics from 11 countries to nominate the ten best films ever made. In spite of the film ferment of the time, the rousing experiments of young French filmmakers, the rebirth of Italian realism, the explorations of psychological films, the critics agreed that *Potemkin* was one of the all-time ten best. Even more significantly, Eisenstein was chosen by these 70 critics as the greatest director in film history.

It is beyond the capacity of the written word to recreate the intense emotion experienced during a screening of *Potemkin.* Silent films, such as *Potemkin,* reach the emotions almost entirely on a visual level. Explanatory subtitles are few. Dialogue between the film's characters serves only as an additional visual accompaniment to the action; the unheard words are incidental to what is happening in the scene. Any attempt to recreate in print the imagined dialogue is misleading and unnecessary. Eisenstein's intent is clear from shot to shot.

This shot-by-shot analysis does not attempt to recreate *Potemkin*'s filmic effects through the use of stylistic literary equivalents. Its approach has been to present an exact description of what is seen on the screen. It meticulously avoids personal interpretation of Eisenstein's intentions or a character's motivation. The goal has been to distill each shot description to its clearest, most precise form, projecting those elements that best transmit the film's story.

Insofar as the medium of print allows, this book enables the reader to recreate one of the greatest films of all time, at leisure and almost as if he were actually watching the film. It can be used in a number of ways. It can be read as pure entertainment with a vivid flow of story by those to whom Sergei Eisenstein's *Potemkin* is a legendary movie. Film buffs and professionals will be able to make an intimate, detailed examination, not possible at a screening, of Eisenstein's montage, directing, and editing techniques. For the first time, universities, film societies, film workshops, libraries, and the public will have at their disposal a permanent, easily handled record of Eisenstein's genius.

All prints of *Potemkin* in general distribution for public showing and almost all prints in library archives have been edited and shortened. In order to make this recreation of *Potemkin* as accurate and entertaining as possible, the original, uncut version of the film has been used. In the United States, only the Museum of Modern Art in New York City possesses this version, without which a study of Eisenstein's editing and direction is obviously crippled.

In 1925, when he filmed *Potemkin,* Eisenstein was a member of the State Cinema Institute in Moscow. He was looking for a film subject which would serve the nation's political goals. The maintenance of revolutionary spirit was essential in a nation that had overthrown its Czar, was recovering from a disastrous defeat in the First World War and had been bled white by civil war. It was a time to portray Russians as heroes, a selfless revolutionary mass dedicated to freedom.

He found his subject in the 1905 rebellion by Russian sailors of the Czarist battleship *Potemkin* against their officers, and the slaughter of the citizens of Odessa who supported their revolt. The rebellion was originally part of a broader treatment entitled *1905,* one of a series of films to be made to honor the revolutionary events of that year. (Another film in the series was Pudovkin's *Mother.*) During a locale search in Odessa, Eisenstein saw the great sweep of steps where a civilian massacre might occur, and his intuition took a giant leap. A new scenario was immediately begun, focusing entirely on the rebellion and the slaughter.

Eisenstein was 27 years old when he started on *Potemkin.* He was a brilliant, troubled man whose interests led him to explore the external, visual world and inner, psychological landscapes with equal intensity. His sensitivity to visual structuring brought him into contact with many varieties of creative endeavor. The art movements of postwar Western Europe and the traditional art forms of the Orient were absorbed equally. He was responding receptively to Freud's theories at the same time that he was working to inspire the Soviet people to greater national effort through his films. Contradictions, the conflict of opposites, struggled within him without resolution. Ultimately these contradictions were forged into constructive creativity. He learned how to use the energies generated by conflict and developed a new film technique that startled the world. *Potemkin,* the film most critics agree to be one of the ten greatest films of all time, embodies these creative conflicts at every level.

Eisenstein, subsequently discussing the organic form of *Potemkin,* stated, "(it) looks like a chronicle (or newsreel) of an event, but it functions as a drama. The secret of this lies in the fact that the chronicle pace of the event is fitted to a severely tragic composition . . . the five act tragedy. Events . . . are broken into five tragic acts, the facts being selected and arranged in sequence so that they answer the demands set by classical tragedy; a third act quite distinct from the second, a fifth distinct from the first, and so on."[1]

Each part, in accordance with the classic tradition, was given a title: Part I, *Men and Maggots;* Part II, *Drama on the Quarterdeck;* Part III, *An Appeal from the Dead;* Part IV, *The Odessa Steps;* Part V, *Meeting the Squadron.* The content and mood of each part differ from those in the remaining parts, yet all five contain an almost identical feature: toward the middle of each, mood and tone jump from one extreme to its opposite. The shift is toward an emotional

[1]S.M. Eisenstein, *Film Form* (New York: Harcourt Brace and Co., 1949), page 162.

state that reflects the greatest possible difference from what had just transpired. Eisenstein tried to express this feeling for the conflict of opposites with his definition of "ecstasy." To him it meant *ex-stasis,* the state of being "out of oneself."[2] This jump of the emotions to the extreme opposite of their normal state was an important goal. In each of the five parts the leap is made at a clearly marked point.

Part I, *Men and Maggots,* switches from the sailors' outspoken resentment over their infested meat ration to their resigned resumption of morning chores. The transition point: an extreme closeup of a cannon's mouth at Shot 129.

Part II, *Drama on the Quarterdeck,* jumps from resignation to revolt as mutiny erupts just before the mass execution of the rebellious crewmen. The transition point: Vakulinchuk's cry, "Brothers!," to the Marine firing squad at Shot 413.

Part III, *An Appeal From the Dead,* moves from the sorrow of the Odessa citizens mourning Vakulinchuk's death to the fury of their demands for justice. The transition point: a closeup of their clenched fists at Shot 727.

Part IV, *The Odessa Steps,* leaps from the comradely love between the mutineers and Odessa's citizens to the slaughter by Czarist troops of the citizens on the steps. The transition point: the title "Suddenly" that precedes Shot 854.

Part V, *Meeting the Squadron,* transforms the Battleship *Potemkin* from victim of the gathering Czarist squadron to victor, escaping to freedom. The transition point: the jubilant cry of the mutineers, "Brothers!," that follows Shot 1319.

In the film as a whole, there is a parallel leap to an opposite state of emotion. The transition is marked by the somber mood surrounding the transport of Vakulinchuk's body from the ship to the Odessa pier. The transition connects the mutiny on the *Potemkin* with the slaughter on the Odessa steps.

What was the revolutionary new film technique that gives

[2] *Ibid.,* page 166.

this Russian film its extraordinary power over the viewer? In the years that followed *Potemkin*'s explosive showing throughout the world, Eisenstein's concept and theories of film form gradually appeared in writing. Like Leonardo da Vinci, toward whom he felt a close affinity, Eisenstein was that extremely rare combination, a daring theoretician and intuitive creator. The Russian director is probably the greatest exponent of creative thinking, writing and directing in the annals of film. His extraordinary investigations of primitive patterns of human communications and their relationship to filmmaking have never been equalled. Today, his theoretical writing on how to evoke intensely emotional audience response is as valid as ever.

Sergei Eisenstein's complete lectures and writings have never been fully circulated outside his own country. Only now are they beginning to be available in the United States. The lecture notes and essays available here yield tantalizing examples of the incandescent atmosphere that must have surrounded his course for directors at the State Cinema Institute. The great interest in montage his films stimulated in the world's film centers and the difficulty encountered by foreign filmmakers and followers in obtaining his direct statements, eventually led to many distortions and oversimplifications of his concepts.

Eisenstein's most important concept was expressed in film language as "montage." This meant the uniting of pieces of film, or shots, not necessarily related to each other, in such a way that their juxtaposition created a new state of feeling in the viewer. The principles of montage, said Eisenstein, were imbedded among the earliest Chinese hieroglyphics, which combined pictures of "things" to express otherwise undepictable "concepts." For example, the Chinese combined pictures of a dog and a mouth to create the concept "to bark." The picture for water combined with the picture for an eye created a new idea, "to weep." In film montage, the director proclaimed, a shot or strip of film that contained a piece of an event, single in meaning and quite neutral in content, was transformed by being cemented to another shot into new and higher levels of intellectual and emotional meaning.

This was just the starting point. Eisenstein asserted that the shot was not an element of montage. The shot, he said, was a montage *cell* that in the mass formed a phenomenon of another order. Montage and the shot were both characterized by collision, by conflict. From the collision of two factors arose a new form of life, a higher level of concept.

Conflict, in Eisenstein's view, was not to be conceived in the narrow, single sense of struggle, but in terms of the broadest effect of the interaction of opposites. Thus the intensity of the reaction to the "collision" of shots and the direction such collision takes is dependent on the qualities of the opposing forces (elements) in the colliding shots. On this level, conflict exists simultaneously in varied forms and qualities. Eisenstein defined these as conflict within the shot itself; conflict within the frame, forming along the lines of graphic directions, scales, volumes, masses of light intensities and depths; conflict between closeups and long shots; conflicts between an object and its dimension; conflict between an event and its duration.[3] Numerous examples of the way these conflicts were applied can be found in *Potemkin*. The principle of conflict between an event and its duration was inspired by a particular sequence in a performance he attended of a Kabuki play given by a Japanese troupe visiting Russia. Eisenstein observed that a fight on the stage was interrupted by a complete halt in the action, a scenic landscape empty of people, followed by resumed action as the actors returned and the struggle continued. He sensed that in a highly charged situation deliberately bringing unresolved action to a temporary halt increased the tension. In *Potemkin,* the Marine firing squad is given an order to fire at sailors condemned to die. (See Shot 385.) The commanded action is deliberately delayed by the director. In addition to shots of the Marines, the sailors, and the officers portraying their reaction to the order, Eisenstein inserts static

[3] *Ibid.,* page 39.

shots, "indifferent" parts of the battleship, a life-preserver, the Imperial crest on the ship's prow, and a tasseled bugle, to prolong the suspenseful waiting and heighten the tension. (See Shots 407, 408, 409.)

Eisenstein's exploration of the possible varieties of montage expression led him to *rhythmic montage*. In this development, the content of the action within the frame was felt to have as much weight as the actual physical length of each chosen shot. Thus it was possible to increase tension not only by shortening each succeeding strip of film in accordance with a plan but also in violation of the same plan. In his article "Methods of Montage" Eisenstein wrote:

"The Odessa Steps sequence in *Potemkin* is a clear example of this. In this the rhythmic drum of the soldiers' feet as they descend the steps violates all *metrical* demands. Unsynchronized with the beat of the cutting, this drumming comes in *off-beat* each time, and the shot itself is entirely different in its solution with each of these appearances. The final pull of tension is supplied by the transfer from the rhythm of the descending feet to another rhythm—a new kind of downward movement—the next intensity level of the same activity—the baby-carriage rolling down the steps. The carriage functions as a directly progressing accelerator of the advancing feet. The stepping descent passes into a rolling descent."[4] (See Shots 970 and 980.)

The Odessa Steps sequence is one of the most memorable experiences in the history of film. The stairway is composed of a series of descending levels, expansive but no larger than many other public stairways. Under Eisenstein's camera eye, the steps are transformed into a never-ending series of stone slabs down which the citizens of Odessa flee with no chance of escape from the massed Czarist rifles above.

In this sequence, Eisenstein distorts real time, stretching each harrowing moment into an eternity of peril. People flee endlessly down endless steps. This is a closed universe structured with fright and the certainty of death from rifle volleys.

[4] *Ibid.,* page 74.

There is no escape, no end to the carnage. There is only the inevitable end for the individuals the camera follows with its darting eye. Eisenstein composed the montage and intercut the separate themes of the Odessa Steps shots in the editing room. From the raw film he held in his hands he intuitively created the sparks that, deftly joined, burst into flame on the screen.

The horror of the massacre is seen through the fate of a few anonymous citizens, most of them first observed standing on the steps anxiously looking out over the harbor. We see a bearded man, a white-bloused woman with parasol, a mature woman wearing pince-nez, her young companion, and a student wearing spectacles. Two elegantly dressed women and a legless young cripple, subsidiary characters, are introduced briefly among the citizens on the steps. Then the camera focuses on a boy standing next to his mother, who wears gold hoop earrings and a shawl. These two are major participants in the tragedy that follows.

Suddenly, the dark hair of a woman fills the screen and jerks away from the camera in a swift blur; the panic has begun. The legless cripple scuttles away on hand-held wooden pads. From that point on, shots cross-cut between citizens falling or fleeing down the steps, the Czarist troops who appear at the head of the steps and the individual citizens who were earlier seen in closeup among the crowd. Eisenstein's montage works with most penetrating effect. The conflict of steps, masses, lines of force, movements, and energies are all bound together by the inexorable descent of the firing troops, the streaming descent of the citizens, the accelerating descent of the abandoned baby carriage and a hypnotic, conflicting, upward march of the anguished mother carrying her dead child. A study of this sequence in the following shot-by-shot analysis yields an immensely revealing insight into Eisenstein's mastery of the medium. One can follow the rapid cutting from one participant in the action to another, the selection of only the most essential gesture and movement to delineate the action, the constant graphic conflicts that energize the story. Climax follows climax. The mother carrying her child is shot down. At the bottom of the steps, citizens who have escaped the troops above are engulfed by mounted Cossacks. The runaway baby carriage careening down the steps with its helpless infant passenger spills violently to the ground. The woman wearing pince-nez is sabre-slashed across the face.

Eisenstein discovered that it was possible for him to create a new single concept from the linking of two unrelated images. He produced such images both logically and illogically in two famous moments at the climax of the Odessa Steps sequence. Shot 1010 is an extreme closeup of a Czarist officer's arm swinging a sabre across his shoulder. As the sabre begins its downward arc, the officer shouts in murderous fury. This is directly followed by Shot 1011 showing the woman with blood spurting from her right eye, her pince-nez smashed and awry on her nose. The image is logical; the woman has been slashed across the face with the sabre. The violent act, though unshown, is as real as if it were seen.

At this moment, with the woman's bloody face filling the screen, Eisenstein introduces a new collision of shots, a confrontation of the major antagonists. There is an abrupt leap from the slaughter to retribution as giant cannon on the *Potemkin* implacably swing toward the camera and two muzzles stare like menacing eyes at the audience. (See Shot 1012.)

Creation through linking works to an opposite effect a few shots further on. The battleship *Potemkin* bombards the generals' headquarters in retaliation for the massacre. Amidst the exploding shells and flying debris, the marble statue of a sleeping lion seems to wake and leap to its feet in wrath. The image is striking but illogical, created by showing a rapid succession of three marble statues, a sleeping lion, an awakening lion, and a standing lion. These three separate shots are on screen for just over two and a half seconds. (See Shots 1022, 1023, 1024.) Together they form a stirring visual metaphor, the awakening anger of the Russian people.

Worth noting in the Odessa Steps sequence is how Eisenstein, improvising on the spur of the moment, dared violate not only real time but the realism of his *mise en scène*. What instinct prompted the director to place a large mirror behind the head of the young student watching the slaughter of the citizens? There was no filmic justification for such a mirror to be part of the scene on the steps. Yet he included it. It had been close to hand, having been used by Eisenstein's crew to throw more light on the actors. On screen, the student's doubled image seems to intensify audience identification with the student's horror. (See Shot 995.)

As he probed deeper, Eisenstein sensed other possible levels of montage structure. The movement within the frame which he characterized as *rhythmic montage* was created either by things or people in motion, or by the path followed by the viewer's eye along some stationary object. When a new element, the dominant emotional quality or *tone* of a shot was added to the other calculated elements, a higher level of montage was created. This was *tonal montage*. In *Potemkin,* the combination of emotional tone and rhythm is clearly seen in Part III, *An Appeal From the Dead,* the transition sequence for the film as a whole. Eisenstein sought a way to cool the violent atmosphere of the rebellion sequence which had just ended. To come were the savageries of the slaughter on the steps. A low-key bridge was essential. The connecting sequence was to be somber, muted, with the chill of lonely vigil gradually dissipated by the coming dawn and gathering citizens. At the heart of the transition is the body of Vakulinchuk, the leader of the rebellion, placed by crewmen at the end of the Odessa pier. Lying unattended under a small tent, the body bears a candle and a placard proclaiming "For a spoonful of soup." Eisenstein's most important criteria for the selection of shots to create the desired emotional mood were their varying degrees of haze and luminosity as they reflect night giving way to dawn. Underlying this *tonal montage* is a secondary *rhythmic montage* expressed in graduations of subdued, hushed movement, the vague agitation of waves, the gentle rise and fall of anchored vessels, the slowly dispersing fog and the random flight of seagulls. (See Shots 630 to 653.)

The constant scrutiny to which Eisenstein subjected the forms of literature, painting and drama led inevitably to creative parallels in his filmmaking. He felt strongly that "at the basis of the creation of form lie sensual and imagist thought processes."[5] In *Potemkin* he employed one such process, *pars pro toto,* the part standing for the whole, with stunning effect. It occurs with the death of Dr. Smirnov, the ship's medical officer, who has previously declared the crew's maggoty meat ration fit to eat. During the rebellion, the doctor is pursued and caught by the mutineers. He is dragged by his feet to the ship's rail and thrown over the side to drown. The final shot of this sequence focuses not on the doctor but on a small detail of his person, his pince-nez, which he had used to deny the existence of maggots in the meat. It is seen tangled in the rigging where it caught during his convulsive struggle to escape. It dangles, swinging slowly to and fro, a vivid symbol of Dr. Smirnov's crime and punishment.

Another aspect of Eisenstein's daring is to be found in his use of cubist art principles on film. He did not identify this montage with such a "Western" term as cubism, but in his London lectures in 1929 on film theory, as reported by Basil Wright, he stated that the best pieces for montage are those which are incomplete. Always, he said, choose pieces of shots that do not fit.

A brilliant use of cubist overlapping occurs in Part I, *Men and Maggots.* A young sailor who earlier had protested against the crew's ration of maggoty meat is washing an officer's dishes. He becomes aware that the plate in his hand bears the inscription "Give us this day our daily bread." Overcome with rage, he smashes the plate against the table edge. The destruction of the officer's plate takes a fraction over four seconds on screen. In those four seconds Eisenstein uses a montage of nine different incomplete shots to emphasize the importance of the act. The montage in this

[5] *Ibid.,* page 130.

scene becomes a cinematic equivalent of Marcel Du-
champ's *Nude Descending a Staircase.* The nine shots
range in length from one-quarter to three-quarters of a second, and in their brief flight across the screen pursue a
nervous, jagged course that heightens the violence of the
act. A study of the nine shots reveals that the sailor throws
the plate toward the floor *twice,* once from above his left
shoulder and once from above his right shoulder. These
cubist overlaps and repetitions of the same act, shown almost simultaneously from different angles, make the audience not only see but vividly feel the sailor's emotions.

Without structure, Eisenstein's montage editing would be
simply an outstanding film technique. Fused into the organic
composition of *Potemkin,* his montage variants contribute
powerfully to the work as a whole, earning it an honored
place among the greatest films ever made.

A Note on This Edition

The frames reproduced from the original version of *Potemkin* for this edition were selected to accomplish several objectives. Primarily it was desired to give the reader a visual background to the shot-by-shot analysis of the film. Insight into Eisenstein's use of montage was another goal. For this purpose, frame reproductions from every major camera setup, plot situation, and characterization have been placed adjacent to the shots they illustrate. A number of Eisenstein's film theories and special aspects of his montage structure have been illustrated with individual frames and one extended frame sequence. A frame from the opening shot of each of *Potemkin*'s 55 subthemes is included to indicate how Eisenstein handled those themes. Such frames are identified in the text as A 1, B 1, C 1, etc. A comparison of the content of these initial frames with that of the shots immediately preceding frequently reveals examples of how Eisenstein handled "leaps" to other levels of feeling.

In addition to shots previously discussed in the introduction, a number of frames and related shot data are worthy of closer scrutiny. *Potemkin* is loaded with surprises and discoveries for the film buff and filmmaker. Some of them are noted here in the order of their appearance in the film.

Part I *Men and Maggots*. The outstanding moment in this section occurs at the end, with the smashing of the officer's dinner plate by the angry sailor. Shots 239 through 246, containing 61 frames, are reproduced in their entirety on pages 23-30 to allow detailed study of this marvel of film editing.

Part II *Drama on the Quarterdeck*. As the crew's confrontation with its officers unfolds, Eisenstein makes telling use of extreme closeups. He instantly characterizes the inner feelings of the individuals he brings briefly to our attention on the crowded deck by using eloquent gestures and glances which swiftly reinforce the tension that builds from moment to moment. Note particularly the frame from Shot 277, a deck officer tensely stroking the strap of his binoculars; the frame from Shot 295, the expression of cunning expectancy on an officer's face; the frame from Shot 346, another officer smiling sadistically as he fingers his mustache.

Dr. Hanns Sachs, the Viennese psychoanalyst, was intrigued by the reaction of a friend who had seen *Potemkin* three or four times and had been "strongly moved at one point in the film without being able to discover what it was that moved him. On each occasion this experience came when, at the captain's command, the sailcloth is being carried on board. In the midst of this operation the head of the fugleman of the guard, called up for the shooting (of the mutinying sailors), emerged clearly for a moment and turned to watch. This watching head seems to have no particular expression, and any expression it might bear would, owing to the fractional time during which it appears in the picture, be lost on the spectator. . . . By looking round at the sailcloth as it is being carried past, [the fugleman] betrays, however slightly, his character of a human being involved in the proceedings. . . . We know that even the guard, in its totality of unfeeling machine, is made up of men capable of sympathy, and we begin to hope."[6] (See frame of Shot 358.)

In this sequence, it is most instructive to see the way Eisenstein splinters a relatively simple action into shot fragments alive with energy. The inspired use of a great tarpaulin to cover the condemned mutineers is an excellent example. The throwing of the tarpaulin over the sailors is divided by Eisenstein into seven shots consisting of five closeups and two medium shots. A frame from each shot is reproduced to show how the director endows the vast canvas with a

---

[6]Dr. Hanns Sachs, "Film Psychology," *Close-up*, November 1928.

menacing life of its own as a giant blindfold for the mass execution. (See frames from Shots 365 to 371.)

Near the end of Part II, note the three frames that show how Eisenstein recalls Dr. Smirnov's lie about the maggots on the meat. In Shot 582, a foaming white circle forms on the surface of the sea as the doctor's body sinks beneath the surface. Shot 583 is a repeat of an earlier extreme closeup of the maggots. Shot 584 symbolizes Dr. Smirnov's fate in his pince-nez dangling in the rigging.

Part III *An Appeal From the Dead.* Early in this Part, great tides of citizenry are shown in shot after shot converging on the pier where Vakulinchuk's body lies. No face stands out. This is an entire city in mourning. Massed ranks move under a viaduct arch. (See frame from Shot 682.) A huge gathering at the pier surrounds the dead sailor. (See frame from Shot 683.) The camera then moves close for the first time to pinpoint individuals among the mourning mass. (See frame from Shot 684.) This shot begins a new subtheme, *Indignation Rises.* Later, the citizens gathered around the body are gradually roused to anger by incendiary speakers in the crowd. The mood is climaxed by a closeup of raised fists that fill the screen. (See frame from Shot 774.) In the following shot the tension now leaps from shore to ship. The quarterdeck of the *Potemkin* is shown in long shot as a wave of sailors runs from under the gun turret and scatters across the deck. The emotion generated by the civilians' bristling mood has been transferred to the triumphant crew. (See frame from Shot 775.)

Part IV *The Odessa Steps.* Note how Eisenstein abruptly sends a chill of premonition through the audience with an extreme closeup of blurred hair and a woman's head jerked in panic. One shot is not enough to create the effect the director desired. The rapid head movement foreshadows the slaughter to come and must be repeated to prolong the shock. Four extreme closeups of the woman's twisting head are used before Eisenstein cuts to the legless cripple fleeing across the steps and through him opens the screen to general disorder. (See frames from Shots 854 to 858.)

In the ensuing action, some deaths are pictured quickly, others are treated in great detail. After the mother carrying her dead child up the stairs is slain, a second mother is introduced. This is the woman with the baby carriage which is to play such an important part in the camera movements that follow its runaway descent. The woman is shot and lurches against the carriage, sending it on its way. Eisenstein prolongs her death to build new audience tension, starting at Shot 960 and lasting through ten additional shots before she falls. The ultimate climax of the Odessa Steps sequence occurs with the five shots ending with the bloody face of the woman with pince-nez. (See frames from Shots 1007 through 1011.)

Part V *Meeting the Squadron*. This part is one endless moment of suspense. The sailors' tense, disciplined vigil is counterpointed by shots of the furious movement generated by the ship. Smoke streams across the screen from the *Potemkin*'s funnels; waves churn swiftly away from the prow. In the engine room a plunging piston races in blurred flight. Throughout, the great cannon of the battleship rear erect as the Czarist naval squadron approaches. (See frames from Shots 1202, 1215, 1223, and 1284.) Eisenstein ends the suspense through a very human device that contrasts sharply with the menacing power of the opposing warships. One of the grimly waiting sailors suddenly smiles and the audience knows the *Potemkin* mutineers will escape to freedom. (See frame from Shot 1319.) The camera angle chosen for the final shot of the film makes it a symbolic affirmation of the entire Russian Revolution. The giant prow of the *Potemkin,* seen from below in extreme closeup, seems to breach the screen as the picture ends. (See frame from Shot 1346.)

POTEMKIN'S SUBSIDIARY THEMES

To help the interested reader better comprehend *Potemkin*'s underlying structure and its inspired editing, each of the film's five parts has been divided into subsidiary themes as given below. In the text, each shot in the film is identified by its subtheme letter and number. Thus A 1 is the first shot of subtheme A.

Potemkin Subsidiary Theme Plan
Total Shots: 1346
Total Subsidiary Themes: 55

Part I Men and Maggots (Shots 1 through 248. Total, 248)

A Odessa Harbor	5	shots
B The Battleship *Potemkin*	2	"
C Matyushenko and Vakulinchuk	3	"
D The Crew's Sleeping Quarters	39	"
E Maggoty Meat	70	"
F The Galley	23	"
G Morning Chores	27	"
H The Mess Hall	36	"
I The Canteen	12	"
J "Give Us This Day . . . "	31	"

Part II Drama on the Quarterdeck (Shots 249 through 638. Total, 390)

A The Bugler	5	shots
B The Crew Assembles	8	"
C Punishment Decreed	31	"
D The Yardarm	10	"
E Escape to the Turret	33	"
F The Firing Squad	53	"
G The Victims	18	"
H The Tarpaulin	37	"
I The Battleship *Potemkin*	7	"
J The Priest	19	"
K Mutiny	65	"
L Vakulinchuk Pursued	54	"
M The Officers' Saloon	12	"
N Dr. Smirnov	22	"
O Maggoty Meat	1	"

| P The Funeral Launch | 6 | " |
| Q A Tent on the Pier | 9 | " |

Part III An Appeal from the Dead (Shots 639 through
796. Total, 158)

A Fog and Dawn	13	shots
B Vakulinchuk's Bier	42	"
C Odessa's Citizens Respond	15	"
D Indignation Rises	45	"
E The Scoffer	21	"
F The Emissary from Shore	19	"
G Ship and Shore United	3	"

Part IV The Odessa Steps (Shots 797 through 1029.
Total, 233)

A The Yawls Fly	18	shots
B The Citizens on the Steps	48	"
C A Woman Wearing Pince-nez	31	"
D The Battleship *Potemkin*	22	"
E A Mother and Son	33	"
F The Troops Attack	17	"
G Cossacks	9	"
H The Baby Carriage	40	"
I The Generals' Headquarters	15	"

Part V Meeting the Squadron (Shots 1030 through 1346.
Total, 317)

A The Crew Decides	19	shots
B The Vigil	37	"
C The Engines	39	"
D Matyushenko	41	"
E The Off-Duty Watch	7	"
F The Czarist Squadron	14	"
G Enemy Sighted!	24	"
H Battle Stations	59	"
I Full Speed Ahead	33	"
J Defiant Guns	19	"

K The Flags Cry Out   7   "
L Brothers!   18   "

EXPLANATION OF SYMBOLS USED IN THE TEXT

An explanation of the symbols used in the text will be of value to readers unfamiliar with film terminology. To illustrate, let us consider a shot from Part IV *The Odessa Steps:*

The legless cripple scuttles down the steps past the two   858 / MS
elegant women. His body, supported by his powerful arms,   **B21**   *79*
swings like a pendulum as he flees. People hurry after him.
The woman with the parasol runs toward the camera until
its white circle fills the screen. *(Cut to . . .)*

The information that appears beside the text indicates that this is Shot Number 858 of the 1346 that comprise the entire film. MS indicates that it is a Medium Shot with the action taking place not too far from the camera. (Other camera positions identified are Extreme Closeup, ECU; Closeup, CU; and Long Shot, LS.) B21 indicates that this is the 21st shot of subtheme B, *The Citizens on the Steps.* The number in italics, 79, gives the number of film frames used in that particular shot.

The words in parenthesis, *(Cut to . . .),* at the end of a shot analysis indicate an abrupt transition to the next shot which begins with the following frame. Other transitions that Eisenstein used between shots are *(Fade out . . .)* in which the image gradually turns dark on the screen; *(Fade in . . .)* in which the image gradually takes shape on a dark screen; *(Dissolve to . . .)* in which the fade in of a new image and the fade out of the previous image occur simultaneously.

To determine the length of time each shot appears on the screen, convert the frame count into seconds or fractions, using the following silent film speed table based on sixteen frames per second.

Frames / Seconds		Frames / Seconds	
2	⅛	64	4
4	¼	80	5
6	⅜	96	6
8	½	128	8
12	¾	160	10
16	1	192	12
24	1½	224	14
28	1¾	256	16
32	2	288	18
48	3	320	20

Complete frame sequence—Shots 239 through 246.

Eisenstein defies reality to increase tension in this scene from Part I, Men and Maggots. The officer's dish is smashed by being hurled downward twice, once from above the sailor's left shoulder and once from above his right. (Pictures read in columns from top to bottom.) For extended comment on this sequence, see pages 13, 14, and 15.

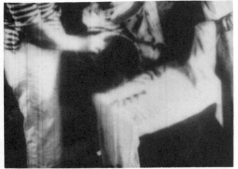

239-1

239-5

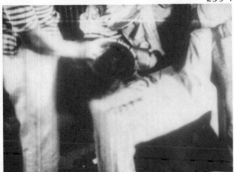

239-2

239-6

239-3

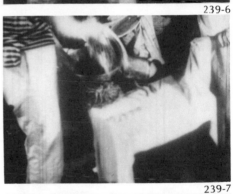

239-7

239-4

240-1

240-2

241-2

240-3

241-3

240-4

241-4

241-1

241-5

241-6

242-4

242-1

242-5

242-2

242-6

242-3

242-7

242-8

243-4

243-1

243-5

243-2

243-6

243-3

243-7

243-8

244-4

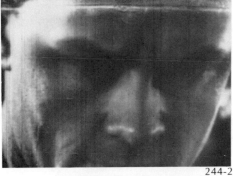

244-1

244-5

244-2

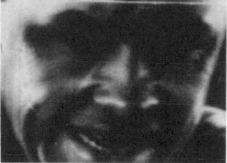

244-6

244-3

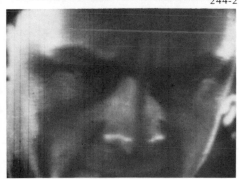

244-3

244-7

244-8

245-3

244-9

245-4

245-1

245-5

245-2

245-6

245-7

246-4

246-1

246-5

246-2

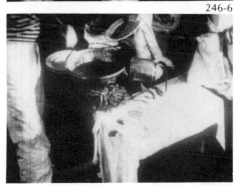

246-6

246-3

246-7

246-8

246-11

246-9

246-12

246-10

POTEMKIN

Potemkin (1925) Silent, 5 reels
Produced by Goskino, Moscow. First showing, Moscow
January 1st, 1926. Scenario and direction by Eisenstein.
Photographed by Edward Tisse. Filmed primarily in the city
and port of Odessa. Some scenes filmed in Sevastopol.

Cast:

Vakulinchuk	A. Antonov
Chief Officer Gilyarovsky	Gregori Alexandrov
Captain Golikov	Vladimir Barsky
Petty Officer	A. Levshin
A Sailor	Mikhail Gomarov

Sailors of the Black Sea Fleet of the Red Navy, citizens
of Odessa and members of the Prolekult Theatre.

1925
Potemkin
Directed by S.M. Eisenstein
Photographed by Edward Tisse
Produced by the First Studio of Goskino, Moscow
Acquired through the courtesy of the Scientific Research
Institute, Moscow and the Reichfilmarchiv, Berlin *(Dissolve
to . . .)*

OPENING
TITLE   397

The most famous of Russian Films, *Potemkin* recreates the
spirit of the 1905 Revolution through the dramatic depiction
of one of its incidents. It introduced a new film technique,
providing a newly conscious conception of the manipulation
of film materials to communicate physical sensations. *(Fade
out and fade into . . .)*

TITLE   593

PART I
MEN AND MAGGOTS *(Fade out and cut to . . .)*

TITLE   156

A wave hurls itself against a stubborn, craggy breakwater
jutting across a harbor. *(Cut to . . .)*

1   /   MS
A1   47

The powerful waves tumble forward over the rocks, seeking
a weak point at the breakwater's base. *(Cut to . . .)*

2   /   MS
A2   64

The ceaseless probing continues as another wave breaks
over the low jetty. *(Cut to . . .)*

3   /   MS
A3   47

Broken, foaming currents again lash the rocks at the base of
the breakwater. *(Cut to . . .)*

4   /   MS
A4   67

Spume flies at the jetty's edge as another wave renews the
struggle between the two forces. *(Cut to . . .)*

5   /   MS
A5   27

"Revolution is the only lawful, equal, effectual war. It was in Russia that this war was declared and begun."—Lenin *(Cut to . . .)*   TITLE   *275*

A thousand yards away, a three-funneled battleship steams across the open sea. In the foreground, a tarpaulin-covered lifeboat is cut by the frame. *(Cut to . . .)*   6 / LS
B1   *40*

A sailor climbs an iron ladder on the deck of a battleship to join a fellow crewman on watch. *(Cut to . . .)*   7 / MS
C1   *98*

6

Seamen Matyushenko and Vakulinchuk *(Cut to . . .)*   TITLE   *110*

(From below) The two brawny, heavily built seamen talk in an excited, determined manner. Their powerful arms fly in sweeping gestures to emphasize their feelings. *(Cut to . . .)*   8 / CU
C2   *35*

"We, the sailors of the *Potemkin,* must stand in the first lines of the revolution with our brothers, the workers." *(Cut to . . .)*   TITLE   *235*

(From below) They come to an agreement and descend the iron ladder. *(Cut to . . .)*   9 / CU
C3   *87*

The battleship *Potemkin,* silhouetted by the sun behind it, lifts gently at anchor on a quiet, oily sea. *(Cut to . . .)*   10 / LS
B2   *29*

The Off Duty Watch *(Cut to . . .)*   TITLE   *77*

11

The crew's quarters below deck are criss-crossed with hammocks bearing sleeping sailors. There is no open space anywhere. The berths are slung in all directions. *(Cut to . . .)* — 11 / MS **D1** 67

A stairway leads upward from the crowded sleeping area. It is surrounded by resting seamen. *(Cut to . . .)* — 12 / CU **D2** 54

Some of the crew sleep naked to the waist. *(Cut to . . .)* — 13 / CU **D3** 39

A bald, powerful sailor sprawls heavily in his hammock. *(Cut to . . .)* — 14 / CU **D4** 43

Three hammocks with their weary occupants swing quietly back and forth. *(Cut to . . .)* — 15 / CU **D5** 50

Another canvas bed, stretched taut by its burden, sways with the ship. *(Cut to . . .)* — 16 / CU **D6** 39

The weary face of a sleeping sailor juts out from the stiff canvas that wraps his body like a shroud. *(Cut to . . .)* — 17 / ECU **D7** 37

A burly boatswain warily descends the stairway leading to the crew's quarters. *(Cut to . . .)* — 18 / CU **D8** 96

A sailor snores open-mouthed in his berth adjoining the stairway leading upward. *(Cut to . . .)* — 19 / CU **D9** 35

The boatswain pushes his way slowly but roughly through the maze of hammocks. *(Cut to . . .)*	20 / **D10**	MS 65
The newcomer glances about suspiciously, searching for any offence. *(Cut to . . .)*	21 / **D11**	CU 46
Like the others, a nearby sailor sleeps enveloped in his hammock. *(Cut to . . .)*	22 / **D12**	ECU 27
The boatswain turns to scrutinize another sleeper and moves toward him out of the frame. *(Cut to . . .)*	23 / **D13**	CU 39
A strapping sailor, naked to the waist, lies fast asleep in his narrow hammock. *(Cut to . . .)*	24 / **D14**	ECU 37
The boatswain pushes past the sleeping crewmen, alert to any irregularity in their quarters. He squeezes his way through the narrow spaces between the slung hammocks and moves out of the frame. *(Cut to . . .)*	25 / **D15**	MS 81
The boatswain approaches a cluster of sleepers. He forces his way between two of the hammocks. *(Cut to . . .)*	26 / **D16**	MS 101

20

Vigilant but clumsy *(Cut to . . .)*	TITLF	*78*
The boatswain's arm becomes tangled in some of the hammock lines. Annoyed, he lashes out with a length of rope at a nearby sleeper. *(Cut to . . .)*	27 / D17	MS *59*
The bare back of a young sailor lying in his hammock fills the screen. The boatswain's arm flashes down and his lash cuts across the seaman's shoulders. *(Cut to . . .)*	28 / D18	ECU *11*
The young sailor awakes with a start and turns in his hammock to look up. *(Cut to . . .)*	29 / D19	ECU *39*
The crewman peers upward to see who has hit him. *(Cut to . . .)*	30 / D20	CU *31*
The boatswain stares truculently at the young sailor, swings his lash with an idle rhythm, then turns and continues to push his way past the hammocks. *(Cut to . . .)*	31 / D21	MS *72*
The young sailor, stunned by the senseless attack, gazes after the boatswain. *(Cut to . . .)*	32 / D22	ECU *49*

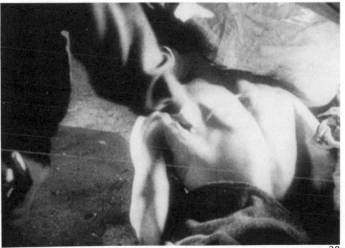

28

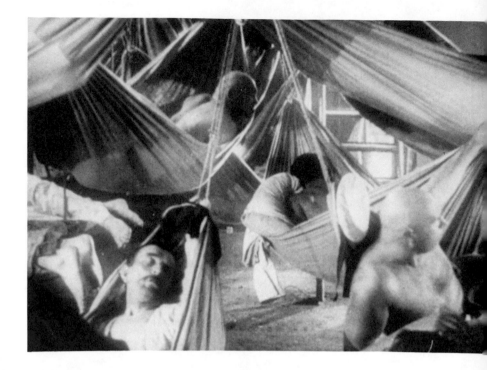

The boatswain slowly forces his way between the sleeping crewmen, glancing left and right as he proceeds. *(Cut to . . .)* 33 / MS
D23   *47*

The young sailor sinks back into his hammock puzzled and humiliated. *(Cut to . . .)* 34 / ECU
D24   *10*

The intruder moves out of the frame. In the background, the victimized sailor buries his face in the canvas. The bald sailor in the foreground wakes and turns to look at him. *(Cut to . . .)* 35 / MS
D25   *71*

The young sailor cannot restrain his tears. His shoulders heave and shake. *(Cut to . . .)* 36 / ECU
D26   *53*

A nearby crewman leans over and pats the weeping seaman's shoulders in sympathy. Controlling his outburst, the young man sits up to wipe his eyes. In the foreground, another sailor casts a bitter glance off-screen. *(Cut to . . .)* 37 / MS
D27   *128*

Vakulinchuk *(Cut to . . .)*	TITLE	*76*

A barrel-chested sailor, naked to the waist, stands among the hammocks and reads from a document in his hand. He emphasizes his vehement words with vigorous gestures. *(Cut to . . .)* — 38 / CU **D28** *53*

"Comrades, the time has come to act." *(Cut to . . .)* — TITLE *125*

Vakulinchuk's arm flails the air as he talks to the seamen around him. *(Cut to . . .)* — 39 / CU **D29** *40*

A heavily mustached sleeper wakes, turns in his hammock and rubs his eyes. *(Cut to . . .)* — 40 / CU **D30** *49*

A second sailor stares from his hammock at the offscreen speaker and nods in sympathy. *(Cut to . . .)* — 41 / ECU **D31** *49*

Vakulinchuk continues to exhort the crewmen with great vigor. *(Cut to . . .)* — 42 / CU **D32** *39*

"What are we waiting for? All Russia is rising. Are we to be last?" *(Cut to . . .)* — TITLE *173*

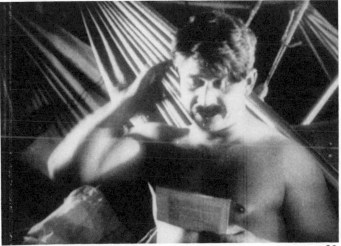

38

Vakulinchuk's arm is a living hammer as it pounds to empha- size his plea. *(Cut to . . .)*	43 / **D33**	CU 37
The mustached sailor shouts approval from his hammock. *(Cut to . . .)*	44 / **D34**	CU 53
The bald sailor turns in his hammock to wave intense agree- ment. *(Cut to . . .)*	45 / **D35**	CU 37
A third sailor adds his voice to the growing support from the surrounding seamen. *(Cut to . . .)*	46 / **D36**	ECU 45
Vakulinchuk, encouraged by his audience, is now an incen- diary. His words blaze with emotion. *(Cut to . . .)*	47 / **D37**	CU 46
The mustached sailor responds to the flaming words, hurling angry approval at the speaker from his hammock. *(Cut to . . .)*	48 / **D38**	CU 35
The lashed young sailor ends his weeping and he, too, shares the determined mood that sweeps the crew's quar- ters. *(Cut to . . .)*	49 / **D39**	MS 45
Morning *(Cut to . . .)*	TITLE	76
A slender young deck officer, his hands stuck indolently in the pockets of his white trousers, steps gingerly around equipment on the open deck. His attention is drawn to another part of the ship. *(Cut to . . .)*	50 / **E1**	MS 159
Sailors gather at an open area on deck near the ship's galley. *(Cut to . . .)*	51 / **E2**	LS 117
(From below) The sailors continue to assemble on two deck levels near the galley. Their actions are agitated. *(Cut to . . .)*	52 / **E3**	LS 49
The cluster of sailors outside the galley quickly grows as other crewmen join the heated conversation. *(Cut to . . .)*	53 / **E4**	LS 71
On an upper deck two sailors move past a door on their way to join the large group. The door opens and a tall, thin, hawklike officer appears. He peers down at the gathering, then turns to close the door. *(Cut to . . .)*	54 / **E5**	MS 160

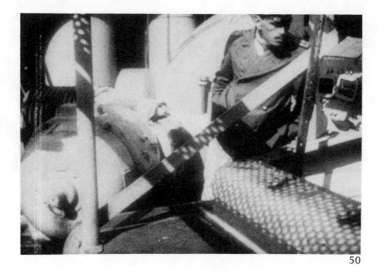

The officer shuts the door and starts walking away from the area where the sailors are congregating. *(Cut to . . .)* 55 / MS **E6** *25*

He hesitates, then turns to glance surreptitiously at the crewmen on the lower deck. *(Cut to . . .)* 56 / MS **E7** *40*

The officer's thin, supercilious face reflects his suspicious awareness of the sailors' agitation as he looks over his shoulder to scan the group below. *(Cut to . . .)* 57 / ECU **E8** *33*

(From above) The sailors outside the galley crowd around to examine a huge carcass of beef hanging from a hook. Other seamen ascend a ladder from the deck below to join them. *(Cut to . . .)* 58 / MS **E9** *71*

As the officer scrutinizes the gathering below, Vakulinchuk comes down the stairway behind him. *(Cut to . . .)* 59 / ECU **E10** *36*

(From above) The sailors pull angrily at the hanging carcass. *(Cut to . . .)* 60 / MS **E11** *50*

Vakulinchuk, unnoticed, retreats up the ladder. The officer is now disturbed by the actions of the crew and turns openly to study the situation. *(Cut to . . .)* 61 / ECU **E12** *67*

The officer walks toward the deck rail to observe the sailors 62 / MS

below. He moves out of the frame. *(Cut to . . .)* **E13**   *45*

(From below) More sailors join the group near the carcass.   63   /   LS
(Cut to . . .) **E14**   *43*

(From above) Sailors examine the carcass as other seamen   64   /   MS
approach. *(Cut to . . .)* **E15**   *38*

(From below) The agitated discussion continues among the   65   /   LS
crewmen around the hanging meat. *(Cut to . . .)* **E16**   *42*

(From above) More than 20 sailors are now gathered about   66   /   MS

the carcass, twisting and examining it. *(Cut to . . .)*	**E17**	*71*
(From below) The seamen mill about the hanging meat. Small groups form to discuss it. *(Cut to . . .)*	67 / **E18**	LS *56*
"We've had enough garbage to eat!" *(Cut to . . .)*	TITLE	*142*
Six of the white-hatted crewmen examine the carcass, angrily twisting and turning it. *(Cut to . . .)*	68 / **E19**	CU *59*
(From above) The sailors pull violently at the meat. *(Cut to . . .)*	69 / **E20**	MS *22*
"A dog wouldn't eat this." *(Cut to . . .)*	TITLE	*90*
The six white-hatted sailors point with disgust to parts of the hanging carcass. *(Cut to . . .)*	70 / **E21**	CU *64*
One of the seamen addresses the others around the meat in a determined manner. As he speaks, some step away from the carcass. *(Cut to . . .)*	71 / **E22**	CU *34*
Two officers approach the galley area and the sailors quickly line up at attention. One is the deck officer who had watched the resentful clamor from an upper deck. The other, wearing pince-nez, is very short, thin, with the pugnacious bearing of a fighting cock. *(Cut to . . .)*	72 / **E23**	MS *33*
The short officer, his back to the camera, reaches up and examines the hanging carcass with a professional air as his companion stands by. *(Cut to . . .)*	73 / **E24**	MS *48*
The little officer continues his scrutiny of the meat, watched by the crewmen standing at attention. *(Cut to . . .)*	74 / **E25**	MS *50*
Vakulinchuk, standing next to the carcass, points to various parts of it. The short officer carefully continues his examination, leaning close to smell the meat. *(Cut to . . .)*	75 / **E26**	CU *77*
Ship's doctor Smirnov *(Cut to . . .)*	TITLE	*86*
Dr. Smirnov steps back a pace from the carcass and ad-	76 /	CU

dresses Vakulinchuk. He points toward the meat with a truculent gesture. *(Cut to . . .)*	**E27**	26
Vakulinchuk glares at the offscreen doctor, turns to the sailors around him and speaks. *(Cut to . . .)*	77 / **E28**	ECU 52
"Throw it overboard!" *(Cut to . . .)*	TITLE	91
Vakulinchuk with grim face waits for his command to be obeyed. *(Cut to . . .)*	78 / **E29**	ECU 14
As Vakulinchuk touches the tainted area of the carcass, Dr. Smirnov ceremoniously takes off his pince-nez and begins to fold them. *(Cut to . . .)*	79 / **E30**	CU 69
Dr. Smirnov's hands punctiliously fold the pince-nez in half to form a magnifying lens for closer viewing. Doubled, the pince-nez are raised out of the frame toward the doctor's eye. *(Cut to . . .)*	80 / **E31**	ECU 40
Dr. Smirnov's eye peering through the doubled pince-nez fills the screen. *(Cut to . . .)*	81 / **E32**	ECU 25
White maggots swarm over the surface of the rotted meat. Dr. Smirnov's pince-nez, a blur in one corner of the screen,	82 / **E33**	ECU 39

come into sharp focus as they are carried toward the maggots. *(Cut to . . .)*

Dr. Smirnov leans back, looks up at Vakulinchuk, and gestures deprecatingly toward the hanging carcass as he pronounces his medical opinion. *(Cut to . . .)*	83 / CU **E34** 53
The doctor's hand and pince-nez tap the maggoty meat to emphasize his findings. *(Cut to . . .)*	84 / ECU **E35** 79
"These are not maggots." *(Cut to . . .)*	TITLE 94
Dr. Smirnov's pince-nez lightly touch the white maggots crawling over the meat. *(Cut to . . .)*	85 / ECU **E36** 37
Vakulinchuk's face is grim and hostile. He leans forward as two sailors behind him watch. *(Cut to . . .)*	86 / ECU **E37** 24
Dr. Smirnov carefully unfolds his pince-nez, replaces them on his nose and looks up. He is furious. His untidy mustache and beard twitch with annoyance as he lectures Vakulinchuk with extended forefinger. *(Cut to . . .)*	87 / ECU **E38** 65
"Merely dead fly-eggs, that will wash off in salt water." *(Cut to . . .)*	TITLE 156
The doctor pronounces his medical opinion sharply to the crew towering about him. His forefinger stabs the air to stop the debate. *(Cut to . . .)*	88 / ECU **E39** 62

80   82

Dr. Smirnov lifts a hanging strip of meat for closer inspection by his fellow officer and Vakulinchuk who stand on either side of him. *(Cut to . . .)*	89 / **E40**	CU 36
Vakulinchuk's glaring face is framed by the raised strip of meat held in the doctor's hand. Behind him the sailors watch closely. *(Cut to . . .)*	90 / **E41**	ECU 37
The other officer reaches out his hand to scrutinize the meat as Dr. Smirnov and Vakulinchuk observe him. *(Cut to . . .)*	91 / **E42**	CU 23
Vakulinchuk abruptly knocks the strip of raised meat out of the doctor's hand. He shouts angrily at the offscreen officer. *(Cut to . . .)*	92 / **E43**	ECU 49
"The Japanese feed Russian prisoners better than we're fed." *(Cut to . . .)*	TITLE	189
Vakulinchuk swings his head sharply toward the carcass to emphasize his protest. *(Cut to . . .)*	93 / **E44**	ECU 27
"We've had enough garbage!" *(Cut to . . .)*	TITLE	93
Dr. Smirnov cannot allow the argument to continue. He turns imperiously and stalks off, as the other officer exchanges heated words with the nearest sailors. *(Cut to . . .)*	94 / **E45**	CU 34
Dr. Smirnov pauses near a stairway, protesting to nearby seamen that the meat is edible. *(Cut to . . .)*	95 / **E46**	MS 61
The deck officer argues with the sailors. He insists the meat is good and will not tolerate further objections. He walks away and leaves Vakulinchuk glowering after him. *(Cut to . . .)*	96 / **E47**	CU 40
As the deck officer strides past the doctor he gestures to Smirnov to follow. *(Cut to . . .)*	97 / **E48**	MS 63
The two officers step through a doorway. Dr. Smirnov turns to shout his contempt to the sailors who have dared disagree with him. *(Cut to . . .)*	98 / **E49**	MS 91

The doctor barks like a terrier at the offscreen sailors. His bad teeth snap. His forefinger stabs. The pince-nez string looped over his ear trembles. *(Cut to . . .)*	99 / ECU **E50** *34*
"The meat is good. No further discussion." *(Cut to . . .)*	TITLE *109*
Dr. Smirnov continues to harangue the offscreen sailors. *(Cut to . . .)*	100 / ECU **E51** *22*
The two officers stand tensely in the shadow of the open doorway on deck, the bearded little doctor in front. Both are indignant over the seamen's attitude. *(Cut to . . .)*	101 / MS **E52** *17*

99

Dr. Smirnov stares aggressively off-screen, his short figure taut with annoyance. *(Cut to . . .)*	102 / ECU **E53** *40*
Vakulinchuk moves truculently from behind the carcass toward the doctor and other sailors follow. *(Cut to . . .)*	103 / CU **E54** *45*
Dr. Smirnov is surprised at the advance. He turns to look at the other officer and his shoulders lift upward in silent question. *(Cut to . . .)*	104 / ECU **E55** *46*
With a slight movement of his impassive face, the deck	105 / ECU

officer beckons Dr. Smirnov to follow him. *(Cut to . . .)*   **E56**   *29*

The doctor hesitates a moment over retreating before the   106 / ECU
advancing sailors, then turns to join his fellow officer. He   **E57**   *48*
moves out of the frame. *(Cut to . . .)*

Dr. Smirnov steps through the doorway and slips behind the   107 / MS
deck officer. His short figure is almost hidden from view.   **E58**   *60*
The other officer rests his foot with calculated casualness on
the threshold and waits. *(Cut to . . .)*

The deck officer observes the seamen with cold rage. A   108 / ECU
mirthless smile passes quickly over his face to be replaced   **E59**   *46*
by an icy, watchful stare. *(Cut to . . .)*

The sailors hurry past the hanging carcass as they follow   109 / CU
Vakulinchuk toward the officers. *(Cut to . . .)*   **E60**   *33*

The deck officer's face is in profile, turned partially from the   110 / ECU
seamen, but he watches them from the corner of his eye   **E61**   *46*
with a hawklike gaze. Then, to show his indifference he
turns his back slowly upon them. *(Cut to . . .)*

The deck officer completes the turn, clasps his hands behind   111 / MS
his back and strolls off along the deck with elaborate calm,   **E62**   *41*
followed by the little doctor. *(Cut to . . .)*

Most of the sailors gathered around the carcass move to-   112 / MS
ward the officers. Two of the remaining crewmen turn and   **E63**   *38*
disperse in another direction. *(Cut to . . .)*

The two officers stand on deck with their backs to the crew-   113 / MS
men. Two of the sailors enter the frame and approach them.   **E64**   *42*
(Cut to . . .)

A group of sailors gathered around the hanging carcass ex-   114 / MS
amine it closely. An officer pushes his way through the   **E65**   *52*
crowd and shoves a crewman away from the meat. *(Cut
to . . .)*

The officer angrily orders the sailors near the meat to dis-   115 / CU
perse. *(Cut to . . .)*   **E66**   *68*

Senior Officer Gilyarovsky *(Cut to . . .)*	TITLE	*76*
A scuffle breaks out between the sailors near the carcass and Gilyarovsky and his petty officer. *(Cut to . . .)*	116 / **E67**	MS *66*
Gilyarovsky stands beside the carcass exhorting the sailors to disperse. *(Cut to . . .)*	117 / **E68**	CU *32*
Another officer alertly scans the disturbance from the shadow of a nearby hatchway. He shouts an order for the crewmen to leave. *(Cut to . . .)*	118 / **E69**	CU *39*
The general scuffle continues around the carcass. The petty officer manages to push away some of the sailors, clearing the area near the meat. Gilyarovsky quickly approaches to back him up and gives a direct order to the seamen to disperse. *(Cut to . . .)*	119 / **E70**	MS *71*
In the ship's galley a small joint of raw meat hangs on a hook. A cook approaches it and smells it carefully. He looks about him to see if he is observed, hesitates a moment, then lifts the meat off the hook. He smells it again as he moves out of the frame. *(Cut to . . .)*	120 / **F1**	ECU *180*

120

In an empty room, an axe lies imbedded in a low circular chopping block near an open Dutch door. The cook enters with the joint of meat, closes the door, picks up the axe and lays the meat on the chopping block. *(Cut to . . .)*	121 / **F2**	MS *114*
The cook raises the axe above his head, brings it swiftly down and raises it again. *(Cut to . . .)*	122 / **F3**	ECU *32*
The cook raises his axe, hacks at the joint of meat, then turns to comment to another cook behind him. He again raises the axe as sailors rush into the galley to plead with him to stop preparing the meat. *(Cut to . . .)*	123 / **F4**	MS *94*
As the cook lifts the axe over his head and chops downward with the blade, two sailors crowd close behind him. *(Cut to . . .)*	124 / **F5**	ECU *45*
The axe-head strikes the tough meat on the chopping block without splitting it. The axe rises out of the frame, then descends swiftly, barely denting the joint. *(Cut to . . .)*	125 / **F6**	ECU *48*
As the cook swings the axe downward, the two sailors pull at his arms to interfere with his work. *(Cut to . . .)*	126 / **F7**	ECU *45*
The cook yanks the joint off the chopping block and swings it angrily away from the two sailors. He puts the meat back on the block, raises his axe, then puts it down again. *(Cut to . . .)*	127 / **F8**	MS *33*
The joint of meat on the block fills the screen. A sailor's hand points at rotted areas of the meat. It is withdrawn as the axe-head strikes the joint without cutting it. *(Cut to . . .)*	128 / **F9**	ECU *17*
(From below) Silhouetted against the sky, the dark, ominous mouth of a giant cannon fills the left side of the screen. A huge swab brush dripping with oil is pushed into the barrel. *(Cut to . . .)*	129 / **G1**	ECU *46*
A sailor sits astride the cannon, facing the muzzle, thrusting home the swab. A hand reaches up from below to help force the brush deep and pull it out. *(Cut to . . .)*	130 / **G2**	CU *23*
The swab brush in the cannon's muzzle is hauled partially	131 /	ECU

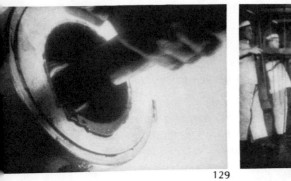

129

141

out and then pressed back into the barrel. It starts sliding out again. *(Cut to . . .)*	**G3**	*20*
A sailor's hands briskly polish a giant winch. *(Cut to . . .)*	132 / ECU **G4**	*62*
The oil-soaked swab slides out of and into the cannon's muzzle, moving deeply down the barrel. *(Cut to . . .)*	133 / ECU **G5**	*20*
The sailor sitting on the cannon presses in the swab and hauls it out completely. The hand of a second sailor helps him at his task. *(Cut to . . .)*	134 / CU **G6**	*31*
Two sailors polish a large metal winch on the deck of the *Potemkin.* Behind them the sea stretches empty to the horizon. *(Cut to . . .)*	135 / CU **G7**	*54*
In the dark engine room, two sailors, one standing, one lying on his back, polish upright metal shafts. *(Cut to . . .)*	136 / ECU **G8**	*47*
Two sailors on deck chip away at a rusted anchor chain with their hammers. *(Cut to . . .)*	137 / CU **G9**	*36*
Sailors' hands rub the gleaming winch vigorously with cloths. *(Cut to . . .)*	138 / ECU **G10**	*34*
One of the two sailors chipping away at the rusted chain grasps the other's hand and speaks soberly to him. *(Cut to . . .)*	139 / CU **G11**	*27*
A giant cauldron of soap bubbles and steams as it is slowly stirred with a ladle. *(Cut to . . .)*	140 / ECU **F10**	*54*

The crew's mess hall. Ten orderlies lower five tables suspended from the ceiling. *(Cut to . . .)*	141 /	MS
	H1	*19*
The dining tables are lowered by the orderlies to serving height. *(Cut to . . .)*	142 /	CU
	H2	*13*
As the tables lower to the proper level, the orderlies on one side turn and march off. The remaining orderlies lean on the tables to position them correctly on their cables. *(Cut to . . .)*	143 /	MS
	H3	*40*
The first group of orderlies marches toward a door leading from the mess hall. The second group begins to follow. *(Cut to . . .)*	144 /	MS
	H4	*46*
As the remaining orderlies leave the mess hall, a petty officer enters to examine the tables. *(Cut to . . .)*	145 /	MS
	H5	*36*
A ladle lightly stirs the steaming cauldron of maggoty soup that will soon be served to the crew. *(Cut to . . .)*	146 /	ECU
	F11	*56*
The petty officer walks past the tables in the crew's mess hall, idly twirling the whistle which hangs from a lanyard around his neck. He checks the hanging tables as they swing gently to and fro. *(Cut to . . .)*	147 /	MS
	H6	*82*
Two mess orderlies approach the tables carrying metal bowls. They spill cutlery from them over the tables. The cutlery is distributed to each eater's place. *(Cut to . . .)*	148 /	MS
	H7	*86*
The petty officer's powerful head turns as he vigoroùsly barks orders to the orderlies. *(Cut to . . .)*	149 /	ECU
	H8	*40*
Other orderlies carrying tableware file into the mess hall past the petty officer to set additional places. *(Cut to . . .)*	150 /	MS
	H9	*72*
The first two mess orderlies finish setting places at their hanging tables and leave to line up for inspection. *(Cut to . . .)*	151 /	MS
	H10	*48*
The steaming, bubbling soup in the cauldron is slowly stirred by a large ladle. *(Cut to . . .)*	152 /	ECU
	F12	*60*
(From below) Seen through a steel grating from beneath,	153 /	MS

three sailors gather on deck and talk. *(Cut to . . .)* **G12** *80*

(From above) Three other sailors squat near an anchor on deck, eating and talking animatedly. One cuts a slice of bread from a round loaf. *(Cut to . . .)* 154 / MS **G13** *37*

One of the three at the anchor speaks emphatically as he holds a dried fish in his hand. *(Cut to . . .)* 155 / CU **G14** *26*

The sailor speaks bitterly to his crewmates, waving the fish to stress his point. *(Cut to . . .)* 156 / ECU **G15** *40*

The anger of the sailors overflowed bounds. *(Cut to . . .)* TITLE *110*

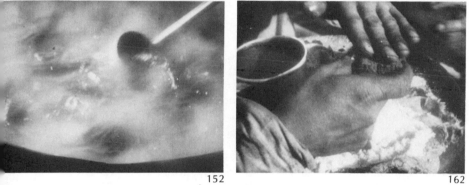

152   162

The hands of the speaker press a massive deck clamp against the dried fish so that he can tear off a portion. *(Cut to . . .)* 157 / ECU **G16** *60*

The speaker's head and shoulders jerk sharply as he tears at the fish held in the clamp. *(Cut to . . .)* 158 / ECU **G17** *22*

The sailor's hand tugs at the dried fish held tight in the deck clamp. He rips off a piece. One hand lifts the vise. The other reaches out to extract the remainder of the fish. *(Cut to . . .)* 159 / ECU **G18** *26*

The deck clamp fills the screen. The sailor's hands have been withdrawn. *(Cut to . . .)* 160 / ECU **G19** *14*

(From below) The three sailors seen through the steel deck grating are joined by other crewmen. *(Cut to . . .)*	161 /	MS
	G20	48
A small dark cloth rests on the deck holding a mound of loose salt and a tin cup. A sailor's hand holds out a piece of brown bread. Another hand sprinkles salt on it and rubs the flavoring into the surface. The salted bread is raised out of the frame. *(Cut to . . .)*	162 /	ECU
	G21	47
The sailor lifts the salted bread to his mouth, bites into it, then does the same with food in his other hand. *(Cut to . . .)*	163 /	ECU
	G22	42
Three metal spigots protrude from a wall on deck. A sailor's hands hold a mug under the right and center spigots in turn and fill it. *(Cut to . . .)*	164 /	ECU
	G23	62
A water mug rests next to the mound of coarse salt spread on the dark cloth. A hand reaches for the mug and lifts it. *(Cut to . . .)*	165 /	ECU
	G24	43
The sailor, holding his salted bread in hand, raises the water mug and drinks deeply. He starts to put it down. *(Cut to . . .)*	166 /	ECU
	G25	67
The sailor sets down his water mug next to the salt mound and his companion picks it up to share the drink. *(Cut to . . .)*	167 /	CU
	G26	42
In the crew's mess the orderlies line up hurriedly as an officer trots down the stairs from the deck above. *(Cut to . . .)*	168 /	MS
	H11	41
One of the sailors salutes as the officer moves briskly down the stairs into the mess room. The others wait. *(Cut to . . .)*	169 /	MS
	H12	37
The saluting sailor calls his crewmates to attention. He is the bright-eyed young seaman who had previously been whipped awake by the boatswain in the crew's quarters. *(Cut to . . .)*	170 /	ECU
	H13	28
The officer halts at the bottom of the stairs and looks around	171 /	MS

while the young sailor salutes and calls his crew mates to attention. The officer acknowledges the salute with a wave of his hand. *(Cut to . . .)*	**H14**	*32*
The young sailor drops his arm. A sullen look crosses his face as he waits for the officer's comments. *(Cut to . . .)*	172 / ECU **H15**	22
The officer stands with his back to the camera. He turns to scrutinize the condition of the tables. He is tall, thin, haughty. *(Cut to . . .)*	173 / ECU **H16**	*31*
An older sailor, barrel-chested, immense, studies the officer like a lion ready to spring. *(Cut to . . .)*	174 / ECU **H17**	*34*
The young sailor watches the officer from under hostile, drawn brows. After a moment, he drops his gaze and turns slowly away. *(Cut to . . .)*	175 / ECU **H18**	*61*
The older sailor boldly scrutinizes the offscreen officer. Then he, too, turns to leave the mess hall. He moves out of the frame. *(Cut to . . .)*	176 / ECU **H19**	*29*
The officer stands with his back to the camera, then turns and moves out of the frame. *(Cut to . . .)*	177 / CU **H20**	*35*
The officer clasps his hands behind his back and strolls past the idly swinging tables as he begins his inspection. Behind him the orderlies file out of the mess hall. *(Cut to . . .)*	178 / MS **H21**	*68*
The five mess tables sway quietly back and forth on their cables, rocked by the *Potemkin*'s slow rise and fall. *(Cut to . . .)*	179 / MS **H22**	*35*
The mess officer approaches a screened locker, checks its contents briefly, then turns again to observe the tables. A bemused smile flits across his face as their rocking motion momentarily catches his interest. *(Cut to . . .)*	180 / CU **H23**	*71*
The five mess tables, each laden with three basins and cutlery, rock rhythmically to and fro like children's swings. *(Cut to . . .)*	181 / MS **H24**	*52*
The officer, an amiable smile softening his hatchet face,	182 / ECU	

sways his head from side to side in idle imitation of the tables' motion. *(Cut to . . .)*		**H25**	*36*
A basin, two spoons and a half loaf of bread glide back and forth past the camera, borne by the swinging table. *(Cut to . . .)*	183 /	**H26**	ECU *40*
The sentimental, playful look lasts a brief moment on the officer's face, then abruptly disappears. The eyes gleam, the face tightens and he continues his inspection, moving out of the frame. *(Cut to . . .)*	184 /	**H27**	ECU *75*
The mess officer retraces his way past the tables. His hands unclasp behind his back as his gait quickens. At the entrance to the mess he stops briefly, turns, looks about for a moment, then leaves. *(Cut to . . .)*	185 /	**H28**	MS *95*
A swinging table with its empty tin basin slides smoothly past the camera. *(Cut to . . .)*	186 /	**H29**	ECU *28*

The Canteen *(Cut to . . .)*   TITLE   *78*

Two sailors stand at an open porthole set in a corridor wall.   187 / CU
Through it they pass money and receive food in return from   I 1   *58*
the canteen orderly on the other side. *(Cut to . . .)*

Inside the canteen, the orderly hands food through the   188 / CU
porthole to the sailors crowded outside. *(Cut to . . .)*   I 2   *36*

Behind the porthole which fills the screen, the orderly as-   189 / ECU
sembles cans of food. A sailor's arm reaches through the   I 3   *37*
opening with money. *(Cut to . . .)*

One of two sailors standing outside the canteen reaches   190 / CU
toward the porthole for his supplies. *(Cut to . . .)*   I 4   *23*

First one, then another arm reaches through the porthole for   191 / ECU
a can of food. *(Cut to . . .)*   I 5   *38*

Outside the canteen, a sailor standing in line looks around   192 / ECU
uneasily and freezes in position. He is listening to the ap-   I 6   *19*
proach of footsteps. *(Cut to . . .)*

The alerted sailor stands immobile with food clutched in his   193 / CU

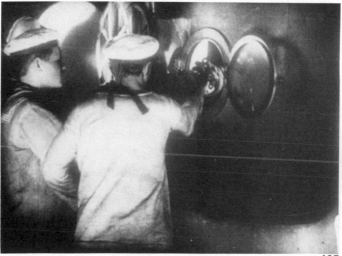

187

hand. The officer, who moments ago inspected the crew's mess, enters the frame and walks past the sailors without noticing them. He stops suddenly, conscious of their attitude, and turns slowly toward them. *(Cut to . . .)*

I 7   *70*

The expectant faces of the sailors are framed by the porthole, seen from inside the canteen. *(Cut to . . .)*

194 / CU
I 8   *39*

Outside the canteen, the officer seems about to speak to the wary sailors. He hesitates and then continues on his way past the crewmen and out of the frame. *(Cut to . . .)*

195 / CU
I 9   *52*

The sailor at the porthole watches tensely as the officer walks off. Convinced that the danger of the moment has passed, he relaxes and turns again to the porthole for an additional purchase. *(Cut to . . .)*

196 / ECU
I 10   *52*

Inside the canteen, one face follows another at the canteen porthole as the sailors continue their purchases. The canteen clerk's arm extends food through the opening. *(Cut to . . .)*

197 / CU
I 11   *32*

The tall, storklike deck officer stands at an observation post on the open deck, scanning the horizon through binoculars. The mess officer hurries up the stairs and excitedly reports the sailors' purchase of food at the canteen. The deck officer receives the news with manifest annoyance. They both clamber quickly down the stairs. *(Cut to . . .)*

198 / MS
I 12   *196*

The two officers enter the empty crew's mess. The deck officer examines each of the hanging tables while the mess officer stands by. *(Cut to . . .)*

199 / MS
H30   *78*

The agitated mess officer wipes his thin mustache with a handkerchief as he nervously describes the crew's actions to his superior officer. *(Cut to . . .)*

200 / CU
H31   *31*

A hanging mess table carrying an empty pan and a large portion of bread swings gently from side to side across the screen. *(Cut to . . .)*

201 / ECU
H32   *45*

The two officers continue their ill-tempered discussion in the mess hall. *(Cut to . . .)*

202 / CU
H33   *29*

The deck officer starts up the stairs leading to the deck. On the way up he turns querulously to give the mess officer parting instructions. *(Cut to . . .)*

203 / MS
H34 *45*

The deck officer crosses in front of the mess officer and starts up the stairs. A baffled expression crosses the mess officer's face. He shrugs his shoulders helplessly and turns to leave. *(Cut to . . .)*

204 / CU
H35 *42*

The deck officer's legs move out of the frame as he hurries up the stairs. The mess officer hesitates a moment. Then he, too, departs from the crew's mess, leaving it empty. The spirit of the crew seems to fill the empty room. *(Cut to . . .)*

205 / MS
H36 *46*

(From below) A sailor reaches up to a steel deck grating above his head and talks through it to two sailors sprawled face downward across it. *(Cut to . . .)*

206 / MS
G27 *70*

On deck, a second cook opens a spigot near the galley and fills his pail with water. The deck officer strolls by with hands clasped behind his back. The cook springs to attention and salutes. *(Cut to . . .)*

207 / MS
F13 *94*

207

The officer questions the cook about the meal that is being prepared. *(Cut to . . .)* — 208 / ECU **F14** 44

The cook salutes again and opens the door to the galley to call in. *(Cut to . . .)* — 209 / MS **F15** 68

In the galley, two hands holding an oar-sized ladle stir the contents of a steaming cauldron. *(Cut to . . .)* — 210 / CU **F16** 34

A cook lifts the cover of a giant soup pot. Steam rises about his face in a swirling cloud. He turns in response to the call from the outside. *(Cut to . . .)* — 211 / CU **F17** 71

The second cook and the deck officer wait outside the galley. A young cook steps through the galley entrance and salutes the officer. *(Cut to . . .)* — 212 / MS **F18** 64

The deck officer questions the cook. The perforated shadow — 213 / ECU

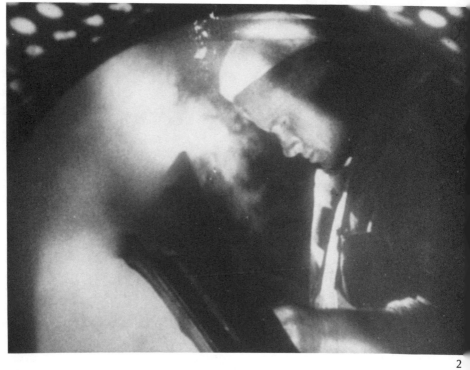

of an offscreen grille falls across the wall behind the seaman. **F19** *37*
(Cut to . . .)

The young cook, his face and chest completely patterned by 214 / ECU
the perforated shadow falling on him, salutes as he answers **F20** *49*
the officer. Behind him steam billows through the galley
door into the sunlight. *(Cut to . . .)*

The deck officer barks an order at the second cook, his head 215 / ECU
jerking with a birdlike thrust. He turns back to the young **F21** *74*
cook. *(Cut to . . .)*

The young cook again salutes. His face is covered with small 216 / CU
circles of light. *(Cut to . . .)* **F22** *41*

The deck officer acknowledges the salute with a nod to the 217 / ECU
cook and begins to turn away. *(Cut to . . .)* **F23** *26*

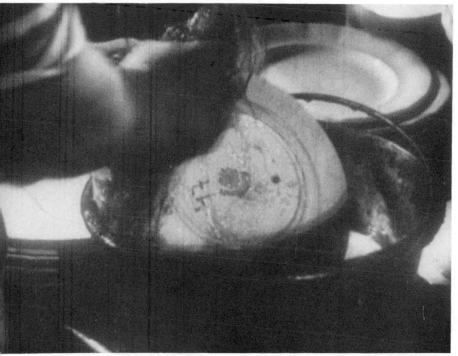

222

A dishpail full of water fills the screen. Two hands are busily scrubbing the back of a china dinner plate with a coarse rag. *(Cut to . . .)*	218 / J1	ECU 48
Below deck, three sailors are washing and drying china dishes around a small table. *(Cut to . . .)*	219 / J2	CU 67
A hand places freshly dried soup spoons face downward on a cloth near a teapot. *(Cut to . . .)*	220 / J3	ECU 53
The arm of the sailor washing dishes in the pail is seen from behind as he gives washed plates to another for drying. *(Cut to . . .)*	221 / J4	CU 57
(From above) The dishwasher hands a plate to a sailor and wipes his nose with the back of his wet wrist. He is the sailor who was lashed by the boatswain while sleeping below deck. *(Cut to . . .)*	222 / J5	ECU 57
Two more freshly dried soup spoons are placed face downward on the cloth. *(Cut to . . .)*	223 / J6	ECU 46
The intent face of one of the two sailors drying the dishes fills the screen. His lips are pursed, his brows drawn as he concentrates on his work. *(Cut to . . .)*	224 / J7	ECU 43
The dishwasher's arm, seen from behind, hands another	225 /	CU

dish to a dryer. *(Cut to . . .)*   **J8**   *50*

The brows of the sailor drying dishes are drawn. His cheeks   226 / ECU
puff from his exertions. *(Cut to . . .)*   **J9**   *49*

(From above) Two hands scrub the bottom of a large dark   227 / ECU
plate being held over the washing pail. It is turned over. Its **J10**   *55*
face contains an inscription around its edge, partially hidden
by the dishwasher's hands. *(Cut to . . .)*

The dishwasher whistles while he works. *(Cut to . . .)*   228 / ECU
                                                              J11   *41*

The surface of the dark dinner plate is being scrubbed. As   229 / ECU
it is pulled from the pail, the white inscription around its **J12**   *54*
edge is clearly revealed. *(Cut to . . .)*

The dishwasher stops whistling as he becomes aware of the   230 / ECU
inscription on the plate, and bends his head forward to read **J13**   *27*
it. *(Cut to . . .)*

The surface of the black plate fills the screen. It turns slowly 231 / ECU
as the dishwasher revolves it, reading the inscription. *(Cut* **J14**   *24*
to . . .)

229

The dishwasher's head moves slowly as he reads the inscription on the plate. *(Cut to . . .)*

232 / ECU
J15 *41*

GIVE US THIS DAY OUR . . . *(Cut to . . .)*

MOVING
TITLE
CURVES
ACROSS
SCREEN *90*

The dishwasher's lips move silently as he reads the legend around the plate's edge. *(Cut to . . .)*

233 / ECU
J16 *56*

THIS DAY OUR DAILY BR . . . *(Cut to . . .)*

MOVING
TITLE
CURVES
ACROSS
SCREEN *85*

The dishwasher's face fills the screen as his lips mouth the words he is reading. *(Cut to . . .)*	234 / ECU **J17** *42*
Y OUR DAILY BREAD. GI . . . *(Cut to . . .)*	MOVING TITLE CURVES ACROSS SCREEN *71*
The dishwasher looks up as the meaning of the prayer dawns on him. He studies the plate for a moment and again looks up, struck by the prayer's content. His lips tighten and his brows contract in growing anger. He looks down. *(Cut to . . .)*	235 / ECU **J18** *90*
The plate rotates in the young dishwasher's hands. *(Cut to . . .)*	236 / ECU **J19** *13*
The dishwasher studies the plate. The two other sailors lean forward as they notice his scrutiny. *(Cut to . . .)*	237 / CU **J20** *20*
The young dishwasher's face distorts in rage. *(Cut to . . .)*	238 / ECU **J21** *37*
(From above) The dish is suddenly lifted in an abrupt motion of the dishwasher's arm. All three kitchen orderlies are seen from the waist down. *(Cut to . . .)*	239 / CU **J22** *7*
The dishwasher's right arm swings up. The plate crosses his left shoulder as the two other orderlies watch. *(Cut to . . .)*	240 / CU **J23** *4*
The dishwasher's head and shoulders fill the screen as the plate completes its upward swing far behind his left shoulder. *(Cut to . . .)*	241 / ECU **J24** *6*
He swings the plate downward with violent force as a second orderly watches. *(Cut to . . .)*	242 / CU **J25** *8*
The dishwasher's head and shoulders fill the screen. His right arm now extends straight up over his right shoulder in a different position than before. It begins a repetition of the downward arc. *(Cut to . . .)*	243 / ECU **J26** *8*

The dishwasher's face, set in a savage grimace, moves across the screen. *(Cut to . . .)* 244 / ECU J27 9

The dishwasher is bent forward. His right arm carries the plate in a swift downward arc from above his right shoulder as the other orderly watches. Again the plate flies toward the ground. *(Cut to . . .)* 245 / CU J28 7

(From above) The plate smashes against the table and the silverware on it flies in all directions. The three kitchen orderlies are seen from the waist down. *(Cut to . . .)* 246 / CU J29 12

The dishwasher is bent far over. Part of his back and outstretched left arm are seen as he begins to straighten up. *(Cut to . . .)* 247 / ECU J30 9

(From above) The three kitchen orderlies, seen from the waist down, stand around the table. The scene slowly fades. *(Fade out and fade into . . .)* 248 / CU J31 62

PART II
DRAMA ON THE QUARTERDECK *(Fade out and cut to . . .)* TITLE 157

249

252

A sailor seen in profile blows assembly on a tasseled bugle. *(Cut to . . .)*	249 / **A1**	CU 26
(From below) The bugler faces forward as he blows. *(Cut to . . .)*	250 / **A2**	CU 28
The bugler's hand and head facing left fill the screen. *(Cut to . . .)*	251 / **A3**	ECU 28
(From above) The long, open quarterdeck of the Battleship *Potemkin,* seen from amidships, is empty except for three officers who stand in a group. Suddenly, scores of crewmen pour out on the deck in answer to the summons. *(Cut to . . .)*	252 / **B1**	LS 110
Sailors begin forming in lines on either side of the deck. Two white-trousered officers move to the left. The third officer moves toward the sailors on the right. *(Cut to . . .)*	253 / **B2**	LS* 57

*Photographed from same position as Shot No. 252 with longer focus lens for a larger image.

(From above) The entire crew has now assembled on the quarterdeck and is rapidly forming into three rough lines on either side. More officers appear from beneath the main gun turret. *(Cut to . . .)*	254 / **B3**	LS* *125*
(From below) The bugler blows his tasseled instrument. *(Cut to . . .)*	255 / **A4**	CU *31*
(From above) The crew has finished lining up on deck. A few more officers join those already gathered and these form a group toward the center. *(Cut to . . .)*	256 / **B4**	LS *196*
(From above) Seven officers stand in line behind a companionway leading below deck. *(Cut to . . .)*	257 / **B5**	MS *22*
Captain Golikov *(Cut to . . .)*	TITLE	*79*
(From above) Captain Golikov comes up the stairs adjusting his collar. He is hard-faced, immense, with a beard that juts out on each side of his chin like the two guns of the *Potemkin*'s main turret. *(Cut to . . .)*	258 / **C1**	CU *40*
(From above) Captain Golikov appears at the stairhead and	259 /	MS

*Using same lens as in Shot No. 252.

258

the waiting officers salute. *(Cut to . . .)*	**C2**	*21*
Captain Golikov reaches the topmost stair and steps out on deck in his long, dark, double-breasted coat and broad shoulderboards. Another officer follows behind him. *(Cut to . . .)*	260 / **C3**	MS *75*
(From above) The captain walks majestically to a position facing the crew, observes them for a moment, then turns to salute his officers. *(Cut to . . .)*	261 / **C4**	LS *94*
(From above) He finishes saluting, again faces the crew, and moves forward to mount a low capstan in the center of the deck. *(Cut to . . .)*	262 / **C5**	LS *32*
Captain Golikov steps up on the capstan. *(Cut to . . .)*	263 / **C6**	LS *24*
Officers in black jackets and white trousers stand stiffly at attention along the left side of the deck. *(Cut to . . .)*	264 / **B6**	MS *50*
The same line of officers is seen from another angle. *(Cut to . . .)*	265 / **B7**	CU *29*
A line of sailors stands at attention in the shadow of the turret. *(Cut to . . .)*	266 / **B8**	MS *27*
Captain Golikov, silhouetted against the sky, observes the crew sternly, left hand behind his back, right thumb inserted in his coat front. *(Cut to . . .)*	267 / **C7**	CU *38*
(From above) The captain stands on the capstan in the center of the quarterdeck, surrounded by lines of officers and men. *(Cut to . . .)*	268 / **C8**	LS *67*
Captain Golikov, with both hands now at his side, speaks. *(Cut to . . .)*	269 / **C9**	CU *40*
"Those satisfied with the food . . ." *(Cut to . . .)*	TITLE	*131*
Golikov gazes sternly from side to side as he continues. *(Cut to . . .)*	270 / **C10**	CU *58*
". . . two steps forward." *(Cut to . . .)*	TITLE	*94*
The captain points his arm imperiously toward the area	271 /	CU

before him. *(Cut to . . .)* **C11** *48*

All the officers in the line stretching along the left side of the
deck step forward. *(Cut to . . .)* 272 / MS **C12** *16*

Three officers step forward. *(Cut to . . .)* 273 / CU **C13** *26*

(From above) A few sailors on the right side of the deck step
forward. *(Cut to . . .)* 274 / LS **C14** *37*

The entire line of officers who have moved forward on the
left side of the deck stands at attention. *(Cut to . . .)* 275 / MS **C15** *26*

Golikov, one hand behind his back, waits with fierce
majesty. He scans the ranks. *(Cut to . . .)* 276 / CU **C16** *79*

(From above) An officer in line watches to see who will step
forward. Only his hand, moving up and down the strap of 277 / ECU **C17** *55*

the field glass around his shoulders, reveals his tension. *(Cut to . . .)*

Two lines of sailors on the left side of the deck stand firm. Not a man steps forward. *(Cut to . . .)*	278 / **C18**	LS *62*
An old officer with white mustache and beard gazes about and repeats the captain's command. *(Cut to . . .)*	279 / **C19**	ECU *51*
"Forward!" *(Cut to . . .)*	TITLE	*78*
The officer with the field glass waits expectantly, his hand moving up and down the strap. *(Cut to . . .)*	280 / **C20**	ECU *78*
Golikov thunders his final command. *(Cut to . . .)*	281 / **C21**	CU *28*
"All others will hang from the yardarm!" *(Cut to . . .)*	TITLE	*23*
Golikov shouts. His extended arm, pointing upward toward the yardarm, is cut by the upper frame. *(Cut to . . .)*	282 / **C22**	CU *5*

Captain Golikov's shoulders are cut by the bottom frame. His entire arm can now be seen pointing upward at the yardarm. *(Cut to . . .)*	283	/	CU
	C23		*60*
(From below) The yardarm of the battleship *Potemkin* forms a gigantic cross at the top of the mast. *(Cut to . . .)*	284	/	LS
	D1		*34*
A young officer looks up toward the yardarm, and a smug smile flits across his face. *(Cut to . . .)*	285	/	ECU
	D2		*58*
Three mustached sailors looking toward the captain turn their heads to stare apprehensively up at the yardarm. *(Cut to . . .)*	286	/	CU
	D3		*41*
Two sailors turn their eyes from the captain to stare upward. One of them shudders involuntarily. *(Cut to . . .)*	287	/	CU
	D4		*30*
A leanfaced old sailor moves his face in the direction opposite to the two previous shots. He, too, stares in apprehen-	288	/	ECU
	D5		*61*

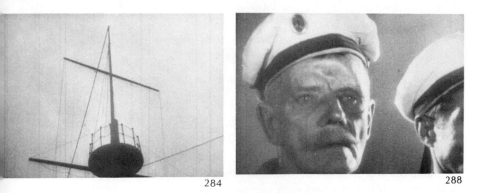

284

288

sion of the fate that faces all who will not step forward. *(Cut to . . .)*

(From below) The yardarm stands silhouetted against the sky. After a moment, six suspended bodies materialize in the air, two hanging from the upper yardarm and four hanging from a lower yardarm. *(Cut to . . .)*

289 / LS
D6 *102*

The old sailor's eyes stare upward unseeingly. The hanging bodies are part of his inner vision. *(Cut to . . .)*

290 / ECU
D7 *10*

Two officers look up at the yardarm. Slight smiles of satisfaction wrinkle their faces. *(Cut to . . .)*

291 / CU
D8 *19*

289

(From below) The empty yardarm stands menacingly against the sky. *(Cut to . . .)*   292 / LS **D9**   *39*

The two smiling officers look at each other and exchange pleased glances. *(Cut to . . .)*   293 / CU **D10**   *49*

Captain Golikov puts his hand on his hip and glares at the crew. After a moment, he again raises his arm and resumes his tirade. *(Cut to . . .)*   294 / CU **C24**   *72*

The face of one of the two officers fills the screen. His expression is sober, infused with cunning. He waits almost with pleasure to see what will happen now. *(Cut to . . .)*   295 / ECU **C25**   *27*

Golikov again orders all who were satisfied to step forward. He slowly lowers his outstretched arm. *(Cut to . . .)*   296 / CU **C26**   *54*

The cunning expression on the officer's face has faded. It is now grim and expectant. He moves his head slightly out of the frame. Only the unshaven jaw, deeply-lined cheeks and slack mouth can be seen. *(Cut to . . .)*   297 / ECU **C27**   *18*

Captain Golikov's face and shoulders fill the screen. Few sailors have stepped forward, and he moves implacably to   298 / ECU **C28**   *32*

295

300

carry out the punishment. *(Cut to . . .)*

"Call the Marines!" *(Cut to . . .)*

Golikov snaps the order. He glares at the crew. *(Cut to . . .)*

(From above) An officer on the quarterdeck turns to a nearby sailor. The crewman salutes, runs across the deck and disappears behind the main gun turret. All the others stand motionless. *(Cut to . . .)*

Under the pretext of leaving the ranks, Matyushenko rallies the men to the gun turret. *(Cut to . . .)*

(From above) Matyushenko exhorts the crewmen around him to action against the officers. *(Cut to . . .)*

(From above) The crewman dispatched to fetch the Marines comes running back along the quarterdeck toward the officers in the center. *(Cut to. . .)*

301

309

forms in front of Captain Golikov, who is standing in the center of the deck. *(Cut to . . .)*

Two officers exchange tense looks and turn to face the sailors. *(Cut to . . .)*

310 / CU
F2   *44*

Framed by the main guns of the *Potemkin,* the sailors stand at attention on the left side of the deck. An officer and Marines march by briskly in the foreground with bayonets at the ready. *(Cut to . . .)*

311 / LS
F3   *51*

The two officers turn to look at each other again. They exchange uneasy stares without speaking. *(Cut to . . .)*

312 / CU
F4   *48*

The Marines continue to march past the sailors standing at attention in the background. *(Cut to . . .)*

313 / LS
F5   *45*

(From above) The Marines line up on the quarterdeck in front of the captain, face left and advance toward the gun turret. Under the guns they stop and do an about-face. They now await the captain's orders. *(Cut to . . .)*

314 / LS
F6   *155*

Matyushenko harangues the sailors gathered around him. *(Cut to . . .)*

315 / CU
E8   *31*

"Men . . . !" *(Cut to . . .)*

TITLE   *68*

Matyushenko turns from sailor to sailor. *(Cut to . . .)*   316 / CU
E9   *15*

"Now!"   TITLE   *72*

A line of sailors at attention exchange glances. Suddenly   317 / MS
about half of them step forward. *(Cut to . . .)*   **E10**   *20*

The sailors begin to assemble under the cannon of the main   318 / MS
gun turret. *(Cut to . . .)*   **E11**   *32*

Other sailors break ranks and move toward the group gath-   319 / MS
ering at the turret. *(Cut to . . .)*   **E12**   *53*

(From above) The sailors standing near Matyushenko begin   320 / CU
to leave for the turret as he continues to urge them. *(Cut*   **E13**   *59*
to . . .)

(From above) In the foreground, sailors are deserting the   321 / MS

knot of men around Matyushenko. A short distance away, with his back toward the sailors, the captain faces a line of officers. *(Cut to . . .)*

E14   *71*

Most of the sailors reached the turret. *(Cut to . . .)*

TITLE   *126*

The area under the main cannon rapidly fills with sailors approaching from both sides of the quarterdeck. In front of them, impassively facing the captain, stand the Marines. *(Cut to . . .)*

322 / MS
E15   *53*

The captain stands on a capstan facing the Marines lined up in front of him to await his next command. As the sailors move toward the shelter of the turret, a group of officers forms a line at right angles to the Marines. *(Cut to . . .)*

323 / LS
F7   *53*

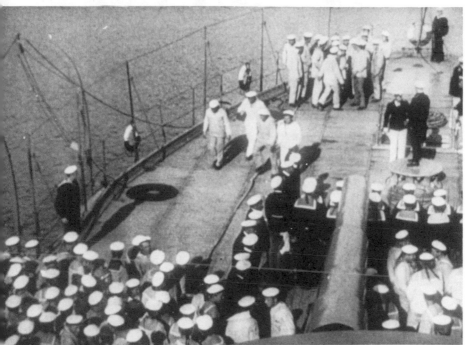

324

(From above) On the quarterdeck, a large knot of sailors remains clustered at the bowrail. Suddenly, four seamen from this group race aft, past the captain, officers and Marines, to join the remainder of the crew under the cannon. *(Cut to . . .)*

324 / LS
G1 *83*

326

327

An officer with an elegant, spiked mustache makes a gesture as if to stop the running sailors. *(Cut to . . .)* 325 / CU **G2** 26

(From above) A mass of sailors moves about agitatedly, their white caps weaving in and out. *(Cut to . . .)* 326 / MS **E16** 43

330

332

The mustached officer turns to look at the escaping sailors, then runs toward the camera with hand raised in peremptory command. *(Cut to . . .)*	**327** / CU **G3** 55	

"Stop! Back to your ranks!" *(Cut to . . .)* — TITLE 94

Some of the sailors standing in the group at the bow instinctively draw together at the officer's sharp command. *(Cut to . . .)* — **328** / MS **G4** 20

The officer runs up to the camera. *(Cut to . . .)* — **329** / CU **G5** 7

(From above) Three other officers run swiftly across the quarterdeck to intercept the nineteen condemned sailors at the bowrail who are making a mass attempt to join their fellow crewmen. The sailors are beaten back, and they huddle at the rail, frightened and defenseless, as the three officers return to their posts. *(Cut to . . .)* — **330** / LS **G6** 242

(From above) At the turret the rebelling sailors mill about in indecision. *(Cut to . . .)* — **331** / MS **E17** 44

Some attempted to escape through the captain's hatchway. *(Cut to . . .)* — TITLE 157

(From above) Three of the nineteen sailors clustered near the bow dash toward the open companionway just behind the captain. *(Cut to . . .)* — **332** / LS **G7** 74

The great, bearlike captain turns suddenly as he hears the footsteps of the escaping sailors. He glares. *(Cut to . . .)* — **333** / CU **G8** 42

"Get away from there, you rascals!" *(Cut to . . .)* — TITLE 118

The captain's face distorts with rage. He shouts, and with raised arm rushes past the camera to stop the sailors. *(Cut to . . .)* — **334** / CU **G9** 54

The captain reaches the sailors as the first is about to descend the companionway. His huge hands reach out, grab two crewmen by their collars and hurl them backward. *(Cut to . . .)* — **335** / MS **G10** 41

A sailor is pushed backward violently and falls at the feet of the condemned seamen. *(Cut to . . .)* 336 / MS **G11** *26*

The powerful captain reaches for the third sailor at the companionway and flings him off as if he were a coil of rope. *(Cut to . . .)* 337 / MS **G12** *38*

335

339

The fallen sailor staggers back to his feet with the aid of the crewmen. *(Cut to . . .)*	338 / **G13**	MS 5
The captain snarls with rage. His mouth is distorted in bestial fury. *(Cut to . . .)*	339 / **G14**	ECU 30
"I'll kill you like dogs!" *(Cut to . . .)*	TITLE	94
The captain raises his fist threateningly as he spits out his threat. *(Cut to . . .)*	340 / **G15**	ECU 37
A crewman listens to the tirade. His brows and lips are drawn in intense awareness of danger. *(Cut to . . .)*	341 / **G16**	ECU 34
The captain turns abruptly and starts to walk away. *(Cut to . . .)*	342 / **G17**	ECU 29
(From above) He strides rapidly toward his officers at deck center. He stops near the companionway facing the Marines and points his arm at them in peremptory command. *(Cut to . . .)*	343 / **G18**	LS 23
(From above) The Marines stand at attention in front of the *Potemkin*'s big guns and face the captain. As their officer steps up on the capstan to command them, the Marines wheel to face the condemned sailors a few yards away. *(Cut to . . .)*	344 / **F8**	LS 41
(From above) A view closer than the previous shot. A few of the Marines can be seen at frame-bottom as they wheel to face the small cluster of sailors at the rail. Their officer steps up on the capstan near them *(Cut to . . .)*	345 / **F9**	LS 29
The Marine officer's head fills the screen. He is smiling sadistically. His hand delicately fingers the pointed end of his mustache. He turns his head and with obvious satisfaction barks an order. *(Cut to . . .)*	346 / **F10**	ECU 26
"Cover them with a tarpaulin." *(Cut to . . .)*	TITLE	117
Two officers hurry up to five others standing at attention near the rail. *(Cut to . . .)*	347 / **H1**	MS 14
"Tarpaulin here, Sir." *(Cut to . . .)*	TITLE	93

346

The two officers stand at attention and salute. *(Cut to . . .)* | 348 / CU
H2   5

One of the saluting officers announces that he is ready to take action. *(Cut to . . .)* | 349 / ECU
H3   19

The two officers turn and start to march off. *(Cut to . . .)* | 350 / CU
H4   13

An officer's face fills the screen as he turns and marches off. *(Cut to . . .)* | 351 / ECU
H5   22

The officers move offscreen. Two other officers from the line behind them now step forward, salute and march after them. *(Cut to . . .)* | 352 / MS
H6   47

The Marine officer's delighted face fills the screen. He still toys with his mustache as he turns to look for the tarpaulin that has been ordered. *(Cut to . . .)* | 353 / ECU
F11   45

(From above) The small group of officers leaves the quarter-deck, passing between the knot of sailors huddled at the rail and the blue-jacketed Marines. Behind the Marines stands a wide circle of crewmen apprehensively waiting for the chill moment of execution. *(Cut to . . .)* | 354 / LS
H7   73

The Marine officer turns his head to study the sailors at the   355 / ECU
rail. *(Cut to . . .)*   **F12**   *51*

(From above) Four officers carry a bundled tarpaulin across   356 / MS
the open deck area behind the Marines. They are followed   **H8**   *80*
by a fifth officer. *(Cut to . . .)*

357

358

(From above) The officers carrying the tarpaulin approach the Marine line from the rear. *(Cut to . . .)*

357 / MS
H9   36

(From below) A tall Marine guard, with back to camera, stands at the end of the rear line. He hears the officers approach with the tarpaulin, and turns to look at it. His face is impassive, but it is clear he feels deeply the awesome role it will soon perform. *(Cut to . . .)*

358 / CU
H10   66

(From above) The five officers stop for a moment as they struggle to get a better grip on their bulky, heavy burden. *(Cut to . . .)*

359 / MS
H11   39

(From below) The Marine slowly turns his face away from the camera and stares straight ahead, again at attention, waiting for the next command. But he is not a machine; the glance has revealed the man under the uniform. *(Cut to . . .)*

360 / CU
H12   31

(From above) The five officers move out of the frame carrying the tarpaulin in their arms. *(Cut to . . .)*

361 / MS
H13   32

(From below) The tall Marine bows his head for a moment, troubled by the impending execution. *(Cut to . . .)*

362 / MS
H14   39

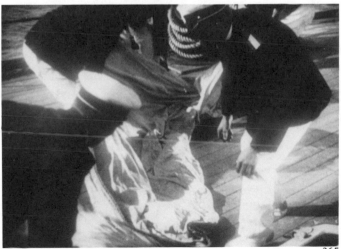

365

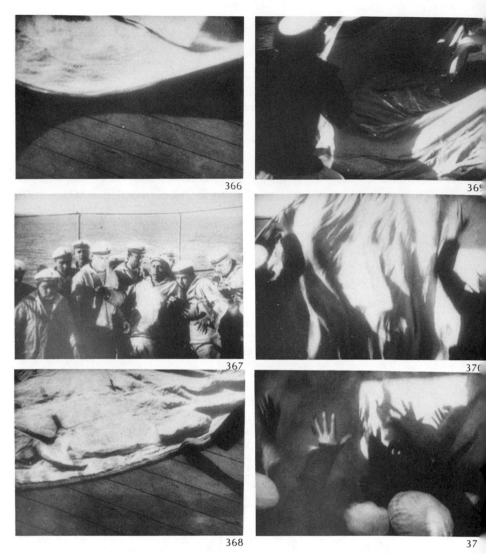

366

36⁹

367

37(

368

37

(From above) The officers carry the tarpaulin around the   363 / MS
end of the line of Marines and deposit it on the open deck.   **H15** *148*
As they do so, the mass of crewmen surges across the deck
to a position behind the Marine guard. *(Cut to . . .)*

(From above) The agitated crew gathers under the big guns   364 / MS

of the main turret and turns to watch the slaughter that is about to begin. *(Cut to . . .)*	**E18**	*71*
"Cover them!" *(Cut to . . .)*	TITLE	*77*
The officers unfurl the huge tarpaulin along the deck. *(Cut to . . .)*	365 / **H16**	CU *59*
An edge of the white tarpaulin settles to the deck like a giant shroud. *(Cut to . . .)*	366 / **H17**	CU *19*
The frightened sailors at the bowrail gasp and back away in fright from the opened tarpaulin. *(Cut to . . .)*	367 / **H18**	MS *54*
An officer's hand reaches out and lifts a section of the outspread tarpaulin from the deck. *(Cut to . . .)*	368 / **H19**	CU *21*
The tarpaulin soars up from the deck, thrown by the officers' hands. *(Cut to . . .)*	369 / **H20**	CU *14*
The condemned sailors stagger back to the rail as the huge tarpaulin rises before them like a white wave and fills the screen. *(Cut to . . .)*	370 / **H21**	MS *15*
The frightened sailors, their backs to the camera, throw up their arms in a desperate attempt to fight off the vast tarpaulin that rises from the deck to overwhelm them. *(Cut to . . .)*	371 / **H22**	CU *13*
A line of Marine guardsmen stands at attention, staring fixedly offscreen toward the enveloped sailors. *(Cut to . . .)*	372 / **F13**	CU *49*
White-trousered officers, seen from the waist down, step back from the tarpaulin. Another officer strides forward and stops near the camera. *(Cut to . . .)*	373 / **F14**	MS *100*
"Attention!" *(Cut to . . .)*	TITLE	*59*
Two officers stiffen their shoulders as the command rings out. *(Cut to . . .)*	374 / **F15**	CU *11*
Five officers, their bodies cut by the upper and lower frames, tense at the word. *(Cut to . . .)*	375 / **F16**	CU *15*

A grim-faced officer snaps his head back as his every muscle responds to the command. *(Cut to . . .)* 376 / ECU **F17** *17*

A line of Marines, bodies cut by the upper and lower frames, stand at attention, rifles at their sides. *(Cut to . . .)* 377 / CU **F18** *11*

(From above) Covered by the tarpaulin, the condemned crewmen huddle near the rail. At the other end of the broad quarterdeck, the agitated crew moves about under the giant guns. Between both groups of sailors stands the Marine guard flanked on each side by the ship's officers. The officer of the guard hurries to one side and waves his arms. The guardsmen take two paces forward and spread out sideways to shooting position. The officer of the guard hurries back to his former position as the other officers move to the side to clear the way for the execution. *(Cut to . . .)* 378 / LS **F19** *245*

The firing squad stand at attention, staring toward the condemned men they are about to shoot down. *(Cut to . . .)*	379 / **F20**	CU *35*
The gaping black muzzles of two giant cannon point directly at the camera. Behind them loom the *Potemkin*'s turret and bridge, empty of men. *(Cut to. . .)*	380 / **I 1**	LS *33*
The *Potemkin* rides quietly at anchor, seemingly suspended between the glassy water and the still sky. *(Cut to . . .)*	381 / **I 2**	LS *20*
(From below) Stairs lead upward to a section of the upper deck. A bareheaded figure in a long-skirted cassock comes slowly into view on deck and approaches the head of the stairs. It is a priest carrying a cross in his hands. His face is barely visible behind his enormous beard. He raises both arms to the sky. *(Cut to . . .)*	382 / **J1**	MS *151*
"Lord, reveal Thyself to the unruly." *(Cut to . . .)*	TITLE	*26*
The "unruly" sailors wait in fright under the tarpaulin, the ones in front kneeling. Only their feet and knees are exposed. *(Cut to . . .)*	383 / **H23**	CU *46*

380

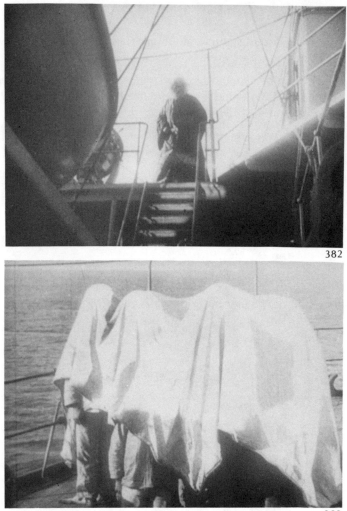

382

383

The priest, an archetypal Russian monk, stands with cross
raised before him, staring toward the sailors. His wild white
beard and mane are silhouetted against clouds of flying
steam. *(Cut to . . .)*

384 / ECU
J2   *76*

The officer of the Marine squad barks his final order. *(Cut
to . . .)*

385 / ECU
F21   *17*

384

387

"At the tarpaulin—Fire!" *(Cut to . . .)*

TITLE   *94*

Cut by the upper frame, the Marines lift their rifles to their shoulders. *(Cut to . . .)*

386 / CU
F22   *8*

(From above) The Marines pull back the bolts on rifles aimed toward the right. *(Cut to . . .)*

387 / CU
F23   *7*

Other Marines facing screen left raise their rifles to their chests. *(Cut to . . .)*	388 / **F24**	CU 25
Vakulinchuk and sailors crowding behind him stare toward the condemned crewmen. They bow their heads, and step back, unable to watch the execution. *(Cut to . . .)*	389 / **E19**	CU 25
Another group of sailors lower their heads and instinctively retreat a step from the volley about to be fired. *(Cut to . . .)*	390 / **E20**	CU 16
The tarpaulin over part of the condemned group sways with the trembling movements of two of the sailors. *(Cut to . . .)*	391 / **H24**	CU 53
Two sailors, unable to watch the execution, close their eyes and lower their heads. *(Cut to . . .)*	392 / **E21**	ECU 46
Three Marines stand motionless with their rifles at their chests, staring toward the tarpaulin. *(Cut to . . .)*	393 / **F25**	CU 45
Three officers wait tensely for the firing to begin. *·(Cut to . . .)*	394 / **F26**	ECU 41
The priest, his halo of white hair tossing in the breeze, waits for the firing. He slowly taps his right palm with the cross he holds. *(Cut to . . .)*	395 / **J3**	CU 65
The cross, now held in the priest's right hand, slowly drops into his left palm and is raised again. *(Cut to . . .)*	396 / **J4**	ECU 35
The officer who had been fingering the strap of his binoculars waits tensely. *(Cut to . . .)*	397 / **F27**	ECU 27
The officer's hand delicately strokes the white pommel of the dagger at his waist. *(Cut to . . .)*	398 / **F28**	ECU 53
The firing squad officer stands with his back to the camera. He turns, looks about him and repeats his command. *(Cut to . . .)*	399 / **F29**	ECU 51
Two of the sailors standing under the tarpaulin fall to their knees in terror. *(Cut to . . .)*	400 / **H25**	CU 24

396

The long black coats and white trousers of the officers stiffen as they snap to attention and wait for the moment of punishment. *(Cut to . . .)*	401 / **F30**	CU *21*
Two rifle barrels stretching across the screen rise out of the frame as the Marines take aim. *(Cut to . . .)*	402 / **F31**	CU *10*
(From below) Four members of the firing squad place their guns to their shoulders. *(Cut to . . .)*	403 / **F32**	CU *31*
Not hearing the sound of shots, Matyushenko slowly raises his head. *(Cut to . . .)*	404 / **E22**	CU *61*
(From below) The four Marines stand motionless, their rifles ready to fire. *(Cut to . . .)*	405 / **F33**	CU *22*
The cross in the priest's hand slowly rises and falls against his palm. *(Cut to . . .)*	406 / **J5**	ECU *48*
(From below) A *Potemkin* life preserver hangs from a rail, part of the great stillness that settles over the battleship as every man waits for the crash of bullets. *(Cut to . . .)*	407 / **I 3**	CU *24*
(From below) The Imperial crest looms on the prow of the ship. It, too, seems to wait tensely for the volley. *(Cut to . . .)*	408 / **I 4**	MS *38*

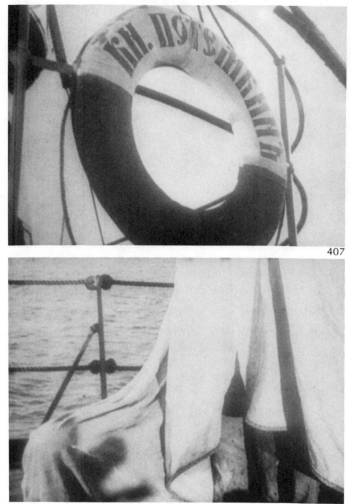

407

410

The tasseled bugle which summoned the crew to the deck now is pressed against the bugler's knee as he, too, waits. *(Cut to . . .)*   409 / ECU **A5** *38*

The strain is too great for one of the condemned sailors. The tarpaulin covering him collapses as he crumples to the deck. *(Cut to . . .)*   410 / CU **H26** *42*

Vakulinchuk's brows draw tight as he sees the sailor fall. *(Cut to . . .)*	411 / **E23**	ECU	*21*
Vakulinchuk decides. *(Cut to . . .)*	TITLE		*93*
The firing squad officer looks about him. *(Cut to . . .)*	412 / **F34**	ECU	*22*
"Fire!" *(Cut to . . .)*	TITLE		*70*
(From below) Vakulinchuk roars a plea to the firing squad in anger and anguish. *(Cut to . . .)*	413 / **E24**	ECU	*12*
"Brothers!" *(Cut to . . .)*	TITLE		*25*
(From below) Vakulinchuk shouts again with all his power. *(Cut to . . .)*	414 / **E25**	ECU	*8*
"Do you realize who you are shooting?"*(Cut to . . .)*	TITLE		*78*
(From above) The end Marine stares straight ahead, grim faced. He may be looking at the condemned men—or within himself. *(Cut to . . .)*	415 / **F35**	ECU	*34*
The Marines faltered. *(Cut to . . .)*	TITLE		*85*

413

(From above) Nine rifles point across the frame to the right. Each gun is pressed tightly against a Marine's shoulder. They waver slightly as Vakulinchuk's outcry finds its target. *(Cut to . . .)*	416 / **F36**	MS *32*
The officer of the Marines slashes the air with his arm in frenzy as he sees their indecision. He gives another command. *(Cut to . . .)*	417 / **F37**	CU *24*
"Shoot!" *(Cut to . . .)*	TITLE	*59*
(From above) Two Marines lower their guns. One stares at the condemned men. The other turns his head to look at the officer. *(Cut to . . .)*	418 / **F38**	ECU *21*
The end Marine stares ahead, unseeing. *(Cut to . . .)*	419 / **F39**	ECU *18*
"Shoot!" *(Cut to . . .)*	TITLE	*77*
Screaming in rage, the officer of the Marines starts running.	420 /	CU

(Cut to . . .)   **F40**   *100*

(From above) The officer dashes to the front of the firing squad and turns to face his Marines. *(Cut to . . .)*   421 / LS   **F41**   *37*

The officer screams at his squad. *(Cut to . . .)*   422 / ECU   **F42**   *15*

"Shoot, damn you!" *(Cut to . . .)*   TITLE   *101*

The infuriated officer stares in disbelief at his squad. *(Cut to . . .)*   423 / ECU   **F43**   *17*

Rifles crisscross the screen as they are lowered by the Marines. *(Cut to . . .)*   424 / CU   **F44**   *17*

(From above) The Marines continue to lower their guns. *(Cut to . . .)*   425 / MS   **F45**   *16*

The Marines' rifles rest in various positions as each man responds to Vakulinchuk's plea and his own deep feelings. *(Cut to . . .)*   426 / CU   **F46**   *12*

(From above) The Marines stand with lowered rifles and confront the officer in front of them. *(Cut to . . .)*   427 / MS   **F47**   *20*

424

428

The Marine officer is beside himself with fury. His pointed mustache quivers above his gnashing teeth as he screams at his men. He raises his fist and starts toward them. *(Cut to . . .)*	428 / **F48**	ECU *14*
(From above) The squad officer runs across the crowded quarterdeck toward his men. *(Cut to . . .)*	429 / **F49**	LS *30*
(From above) The officer rushes at a Marine standing with lowered rifle, grabs it violently and tries to wrench it from his hands. *(Cut to . . .)*	430 / **F50**	CU *42*
Vakulinchuk, surrounded by fellow crewmen, points the way. *(Cut to . . .)*	431 / **E26**	CU *14*
"To the rifles, brothers!" *(Cut to . . .)*	TITLE	*86*
Vakulinchuk lunges forward with arms raised, leading the revolt. *(Cut to . . .)*	432 / **E27**	CU *9*
The members of the firing squad start to point their rifles upward. *(Cut to . . .)*	433 / **F51**	MS *6*
Vakulinchuk roars out a command to the crewmen and darts away. *(Cut to . . .)*	434 / **E28**	ECU *17*
(From above) Vakulinchuk climbs up the side of the main	435 /	MS

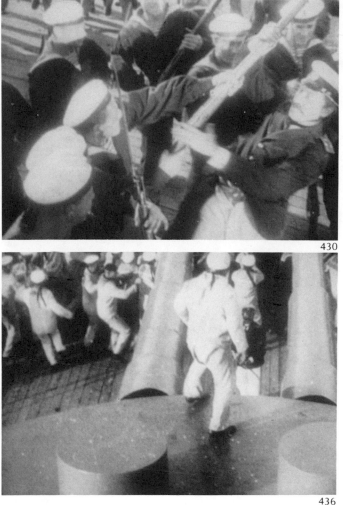

430

436

gun turret and scrambles to its flat, circular top. *(Cut to . . .)*   **E29**   *24*

(From above) Vakulinchuk stands upright on the turret and looks down at the milling crewmen on the quarterdeck. *(Cut to . . .)*   436 / LS   **E30**   *16*

Vakulinchuk raises his hands and shouts to the sailors below.   437 / CU

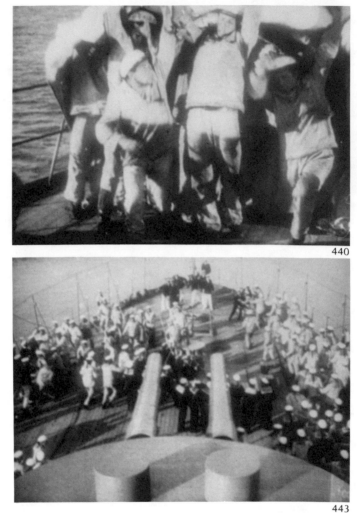

440

443

Vakulinchuk hurls the incendiary demand at the crew. *(Cut to . . .)*	439 / ECU **E33**	8
The condemned men under the tarpaulin hear the cries and fling the cover off their heads. *(Cut to . . .)*	440 / MS **H27**	14
The tarpaulin fills the screen momentarily before it drops to the deck. The freed sailors begin to scatter. *(Cut to . . .)*	441 / CU **H28**	17
The condemned men start running toward the crew massed under the giant cannon. *(Cut to . . .)*	442 / MS **H29**	18
(From above) The entire quarterdeck of the *Potemkin* swarms with men. The suddenly liberated sailors race toward the turret as the crew surrounds the officers and overruns the deck. *(Cut to . . .)*	443 / LS **K1**	32
(From above) The officer struggling for possession of a Marine's rifle is enveloped by his squad. He is whirled around and thrown off balance. *(Cut to . . .)*	444 / CU **F52**	40
The last four condemned sailors race from the fallen tarpaulin. *(Cut to . . .)*	445 / MS **H30**	10

447

The Marines surge forward with upraised rifles. *(Cut to . . .)*	446 / **F53**	CU *11*

The tarpaulin lies in soft folds on the deck, no longer a terrifying shroud. The wind catches it. For a moment it swells as if to follow the escaped men, then sinks back	447 / **H31**	MS *70*

448

450

deflated. *(Cut to . . .)*

Seamen struggle with their officers. Arms flail, officers are beaten to their knees, hands tear at uniforms in a wild melee. *(Cut to . . .)*	448 / **K2**	MS 24
(From above) The bodies of sailors and officers swirl about, locked in struggle. *(Cut to . . .)*	449 / **K3**	CU 21
(From directly overhead) Sailors on different deck levels race by in opposite directions. *(Cut to . . .)*	450 / **K4**	LS 57
(From beneath) The flag of the battleship *Potemkin* waves triumphantly from its staff. *(Cut to . . .)*	451 / **I 5**	CU 28
A ring of sailors rains blows on a few surrounded officers. *(Cut to . . .)*	452 / **K5**	CU 42
An officer breaks away from the scuffle on deck and runs toward the captain's companionway leading to a lower level. *(Cut to . . .)*	453 / **K6**	MS 29
(From above) On the quarterdeck of the *Potemkin* the sailors swirl like a breaking wave over groups of officers, enveloping them. *(Cut to . . .)*	454 / **K7**	LS 20

458

(From directly overhead) Larger groups of sailors, some armed, race by in opposite directions on two different deck levels. *(Cut to . . .)*	455 / **K8**	LS *37*
Five sailors hurry into a guard room where rifles are stacked. *(Cut to . . .)*	456 / **K9**	MS *41*
A forest of bayonets lines the wall. A sailor rushes up and reaches for two of the rifles. *(Cut to . . .)*	457 / **K10**	CU *18*
A sailor's bare foot is seen in front of a line of rifle butts against the wall. A rifle butt moves across the screen as the weapon is removed from its rack. *(Cut to . . .)*	458 / **K11**	ECU *10*
A line of seven bayonets rises like bars through the frame. As the head of a sailor moves into the frame, two of the weapons are removed from the rack. *(Cut to . . .)*	459 / **K12**	ECU *25*
The five sailors take positions near rifles in a narrow corridor lined with weapons. *(Cut to . . .)*	460 / **K13**	MS *23*
Four rifle muzzles stand in a row, bayonets attached. Hands reach out and remove the second and the fourth. *(Cut to . . .)*	461 / **K14**	ECU *15*
Six rifle butts rest in their holders on the floor, next to a sailor's bare foot. The fifth and sixth rifles are pulled out and handed on. *(Cut to . . .)*	462 / **K15**	ECU *12*
Each sailor in the weapons corridor rushes out as he obtains a rifle. Others come in. *(Cut to . . .)*	463 / **K16**	MS *24*
(From above) Fighting rages near the captain's companion-way on the quarterdeck. As an officer runs down the steps, the *Potemkin*'s captain lumbers after him. Two sailors rush to the stairs and grasp the captain's arms to prevent his escape. *(Cut to . . .)*	464 / **K17**	MS *60*
An officer doubles over as three sailors pound his head and knock off his hat. *(Cut to . . .)*	465 / **K18**	CU *34*
(From above) At the companionway, the captain shakes off his pursuers and sends them flying backward with a heave of his powerful arms. *(Cut to . . .)*	466 / **K19**	MS *26*

466

A struggling group seen from the hips down tramples the tarpaulin as they fight. *(Cut to . . .)* — 467 / MS **H32** *38*

(From above) A half-dozen sailors and officers struggle frantically in a melee of flailing arms. *(Cut to . . .)* — 468 / CU **K20** *37*

(From below) The wildly flapping flag of the *Potemkin* fills the screen. *(Cut to . . .)* — 469 / CU **I 6** *17*

(From above) At the companionway, the captain, freed of his pursuers, hurries down the steps. An officer about to follow him is thrown to the deck by a lunging sailor. *(Cut to . . .)* — 470 / MS **K21** *35*

(From directly overhead) Newly armed sailors on two deck levels now race to rejoin the struggle. *(Cut to . . .)* — 471 / LS **K22** *50*

On deck, an officer is knocked down and falls on the tarpaulin. *(Cut to . . .)* — 472 / CU **H33** *23*

In the weapons storeroom, a porthole swings open and a sailor shouts through the opening to another crewman near the stacked rifles. *(Cut to . . .)* — 473 / CU **K23** *20*

The crewman by the weapons reaches for two of the rifles and steps toward the porthole. *(Cut to . . .)* — 474 / CU **K24** *20*

A rifle is passed butt first through the porthole to the sailor on the other side. *(Cut to . . .)*	475 / **K25**	ECU *26*
A sailor's bare foot is seen beside a six-gun rifle rack. The third and fourth rifles are lifted from their places and passed on. *(Cut to . . .)*	476 / **K26**	ECU *16*
A sailor's face appears at the porthole in the weapons store-room. He shouts excitedly to another crewman within. A hand reaches for a rifle with bayonet attached standing on a rack. *(Cut to . . .)*	477 / **K27**	ECU *17*
A sailor's bare foot is seen beside the rifle rack. The first and second rifles are lifted from their places and passed out of the frame. *(Cut to . . .)*	478 / **K28**	ECU *19*
A sailor hurries from the weapons storeroom with two rifles in his hand. *(Cut to . . .)*	479 / **K29**	MS *13*
The officer thrown on the tarpaulin struggles with his assailants. His white cap falls off. Suddenly the sailors begin folding the tarpaulin around his body. *(Cut to . . .)*	480 / **H34**	CU *20*
The officer in the tarpaulin is quickly trussed in its folds by the sailors. *(Cut to . . .)*	481 / **H35**	CU *18*
The sailors begin to lift the writhing figure of the ensnared officer. His free hand frantically catches at a sailor's leg. *(Cut to . . .)*	482 / **H36**	CU *28*
(From above) Vakulinchuk races along a metal runway on an upper deck, pursued closely by an officer armed with a	483 / **L1**	MS *123*

483

rifle. He grasps a wire halyard, swings across an open area and scrambles, crablike, to the top of a domed ventilator. He and the officer face each other momentarily. *(Cut to . . .)*

On the far side of the ventilator, Vakulinchuk squirms around and starts sliding off the domed crown headfirst, using an iron pipe as a support. *(Cut to . . .)*	484 / MS L2 32
(From above) On a stairway leading to the upper deck, a hand emerges slowly into the sunlight, bearing a large metal crucifix. *(Cut to . . .)*	485 / CU J6 30
An elaborately engraved crucifix stands in front of a patterned shadow cast by the metal runway. *(Cut to . . .)*	486 / ECU J7 26
Vakulinchuk hesitates on the domed ventilator as he sees the crucifix and the priest rising into view. He is caught between the cross before him and the officer pursuing him. *(Cut to . . .)*	487 / MS J8 27
(From above) The awesome looking priest holds high a crucifix and slowly mounts the stairway leading to the upper level. His face and head are almost covered by a thick white mane and beard that radiate wildly outward. *(Cut to . . .)*	488 / CU J9 39
Vakulinchuk leans forward to stare at the oncoming priest.	489 / ECU

488

The pursuing officer is behind him. *(Cut to . . .)* **L3** *22*

The priest's head, like that of some dreaded god, fills the 490 / ECU
screen. The cross is held high before him. He speaks. *(Cut* **J10** *23*
to . . .)

"You are fighting God." *(Cut to . . .)* TITLE *85*

494

The stormy face of the priest sternly abjures the sailor. *(Cut to . . .)* 491 / ECU J11 25

The crucifix fills the screen against a dappled light and dark background. *(Cut to . . .)* 492 / ECU J12 12

(From close above) Sailors' caps and officers' hats weave in an angry dance as the general struggle continues on deck. *(Cut to . . .)* 493 / CU K30 11

(From above) The deck of the *Potemkin* is covered with a squirming, struggling mass of sailors pushing forward against the officers. *(Cut to . . .)* 494 / LS K31 33

Vakulinchuk, kneeling on the ventilator, watches the priest slowly approach and move his crucifix through the air in the sacred pattern of the cross. *(Cut to . . .)* 495 / CU J13 43

"Away with you, Chaldean!" *(Cut to. . .)* TITLE 94

As the priest waves his crucifix, Vakulinchuk leaps at him from the ventilator. *(Cut to . . .)* 496 / CU L4 30

The priest is hurled backward to the metal runway. Vakulinchuk grabs him by his collar. *(Cut to . . .)* 497 / CU L5 33

As Vakulinchuk leans over the priest, he realizes that the armed officer has come up behind him. He starts to straighten up. *(Cut to . . .)* 498 / MS L6 14

Vakulinchuk swings his arm to fend off the rifle butt thrust at him by the officer. *(Cut to . . .)* 499 / CU L7 4

Vakulinchuk, fighting for possession of the officer's rifle, is forced backward against the ventilator. *(Cut to . . .)* 500 / CU L8 34

On the quarterdeck, a few sailors try to pin down an officer who has just been thrown to the deck. *(Cut to . . .)* 501 / CU K32 21

The officer trussed in the tarpaulin is pulled along the quarterdeck by a group of sailors. *(Cut to . . .)* 502 / CU H37 18

The officer who has just been knocked down is also dragged along the deck. His right leg is tangled in a tarpaulin and he clutches at deck fittings as he is hauled. *(Cut to . . .)* 503 / CU K33 33

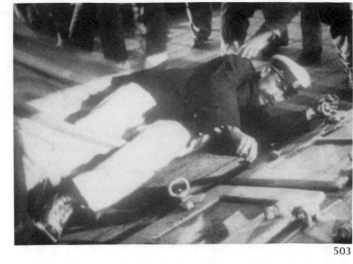

503

Vakulinchuk and the officer, locked in struggle for the rifle, twist about near the ventilator. *(Cut to . . .)*

504 / CU
L9   21

Vakulinchuk and the officer wrench savagely at the rifle between them. Their shoulders fill the screen. *(Cut to . . .)*

505 / ECU
L10   38

On the quarterdeck, the sailors hauling the officer along the deck rip his hands from their grip on the deck fittings. *(Cut to . . .)*

506 / CU
K34   37

Three steps of a metal stairway slant upward across the screen. A sailor's feet hurry down the steps. *(Cut to . . .)*

507 / ECU
K35   7

(From below) A sailor races down the metal stairway. *(Cut to . . .)*

508 / CU
K36   5

A sailor's feet swiftly descend the metal steps of the stairway. *(Cut to . . .)*

509 / ECU
K37   15

On the upper deck, Vakulinchuk and the officer continue to struggle for possession of the rifle. In the background, the priest waves his crucifix. *(Cut to . . .)*

510 / MS
L11   12

Vakulinchuk and the officer, off-balance, swerve in front of the priest. *(Cut to . . .)*

511 / MS
L12   11

(From above) On the quarterdeck of the *Potemkin* over sixty crewmen and officers are embroiled in a full-scale

512 / LS
K38   22

514

struggle. *(Cut to . . .)*

The officer struggling with Vakulinchuk slips momentarily to the gangway. He regains his footing, still clutching his rifle, but Vakulinchuk sends him sprawling. The unarmed sailor turns toward the priest. *(Cut to . . .)*	513 / L13	MS *55*
The crucifix flies toward the deck and one of its trefoiled arms imbeds itself like a dagger in the wood. *(Cut to . . .)*	514 / J14	CU *10*
The priest starts falling backward down the stairway on which he has been standing. Vakulinchuk's legs are seen at the head of the stairs. *(Cut to . . .)*	515 / J15	MS *19*
(From above) Staring upward, the priest falls backward down the stairway. *(Cut to . . .)*	516 / J16	CU *14*
The priest's twisted body lies crushed against a wall at the bottom of the steps. He looks upward, dazed, arms spread wide. *(Cut to . . .)*	517 / J17	CU *23*
As the officer lunges again at Vakulinchuk, the sailor starts down the stairway toward the priest. *(Cut to . . .)*	518 / L14	MS *15*
Vakulinchuk runs down the steps. *(Cut to . . .)*	519 / L15	MS *19*
At the foot of the stairs, Vakulinchuk leaps over the prostrate	520 /	CU

figure of the priest and peers upward to see if the officer has followed him. *(Cut to . . .)*	**L16**	*32*
At the head of the stairs, the officer starts down with rifle in hand. *(Cut to . . .)*	521 / **L17**	MS *18*
Vakulinchuk looks quickly over his shoulder for an escape route. *(Cut to . . .)*	522 / **L18**	CU *13*
The crucifix stands imbedded in the deck. *(Cut to . . .)*	523 / **J18**	CU *29*
Vakulinchuk hurriedly glances left and right and then runs off. *(Cut to . . .)*	524 / **L19**	CU *31*
At another part of the ship, a half-dozen armed sailors descend an open stairway and run along the deck past a door. After they have gone by, an officer exits from the doorway, sees them disappear and escapes in the opposite direction. *(Cut to . . .)*	525 / **K39**	MS *104*
(From below) Three armed sailors hurry down a deck stairway. *(Cut to . . .)*	526 / **K40**	CU *29*
Three white candlesticks crown an elaborate candelabra affixed to a piano. *(Cut to . . .)*	527 / **M1**	ECU *7*
In the officers' salon an upright piano decorated with two candelabra stands against the wall. An officer grapples with a sailor, hurls him to the floor, and climbs up on the piano.	528 / **M2**	MS *41*

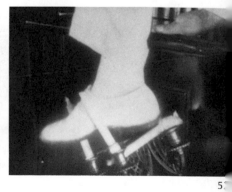

527   5

533

(Cut to . . .)

The officer's white shoe steps hard on the keys of the piano. The other shoe moves past swiftly as he clambers to the top. *(Cut to . . .)*

529 / ECU
M3 30

The officer's white shoe crushes the three white candles as he steps on the candelabra while turning to face the sailor. *(Cut to . . .)*

530 / ECU
M4 17

Straddling the piano, the officer fires a revolver at the sailor running past to escape the shot. *(Cut to . . .)*

531 / MS
M5 13

The officer holds his smoking pistol and watches. *(Cut to . . .)*

532 / CU
M6 22

Two sailors rush into the salon. One hauls the officer from his perch on the piano and sends him flying head over heels against a large easy chair. The first sailor, untouched, joins them. *(Cut to . . .)*

533 / MS
M7 68

(From above) At a gun turret extending over the water, two sailors close in on an officer who has climbed out to a precarious perch. He backs away, reaching for the cannon barrel. *(Cut to . . .)*

534 / MS
K41 14

The officer loses his footing but saves himself from falling

535 / CU

into the water by clutching the barrel behind him with both **K42**   24
hands. He hangs as if crucified. *(Cut to . . .)*

In the salon, the sailors lift the officer and smash his body   536 / MS
down against the easy chair. They pound him with their fists.   **M8**   42
(Cut to . . .)

At the turret, the officer climbs up on the gun barrel and   537 / CU
tries to escape from the two sailors, who follow him. *(Cut*   **K43**   71
to . . .)

(From above) The officer, pursued by the two sailors, climbs   538 / CU
up a series of metal rungs. Above him, a sailor's foot ap-   **K44**   87
pears. The officer is surrounded and overwhelmed. *(Cut*
to . . .)

In the salon, the sailors pummel the officer in the chair.   539 / CU
Behind them another officer and sailor move into view,   **M9**   39
locked in desperate struggle. *(Cut to . . .)*

Two other sailors join the attack on the officer in the salon.   540 / MS
Though assailed from all sides, he manages to climb up on   **M10**   83
the piano stool. *(Cut to . . .)*

542

(From below) Armed sailors on deck race up an iron stairway. *(Cut to . . .)*   541 / CU   **K45**   *21*

The officer on the gun turret ladder rungs is clawed at by crewmen. A sailor waiting above the officer stamps down at his head. The officer falls backward into another sailor's grasp. *(Cut to . . .)*   542 / MS   **K46**   *51*

In the salon, a sailor seizes the officer by the shoulders and spins him over like a wheel. Another sailor smashes the piano stool down on him. *(Cut to . . .)*   543 / MS   **M11**   *63*

(From directly above) The officer at the turret, flung by the sailors, soars through the air head first in a great arc toward the ocean below. *(Cut to . . .)*   544 / CU   **K47**   *17*

The officer falls in a slow somersault, his dark jacket and white trousers wheeling through the air. He hits the water with a great splash. White foam spreads rapidly. *(Cut to . . .)*   545 / LS   **K48**   *44*

The officer's head and arm break through the foaming circle as he surfaces momentarily. *(Cut to . . .)*   546 / MS   **K49**   *32*

545

A life preserver hangs on a deck rail. *(Cut to . . .)*	547 /	CU
	I 7	*24*

Armed sailors stream past on the quarterdeck, dodging under the giant cannon that juts from the main turret. *(Cut to . . .)* — 548 / MS **K50** *72*

(From below) A sailor's arms and shoulders swing swiftly through the air. *(Cut to . . .)* — 549 / ECU **K51** *9*

(From below) Holding the barrel of his rifle, the sailor swings the weapon downward like a pickaxe. *(Cut to . . .)* — 550 / CU **K52** *6*

(From below) The muzzle of a cannon stretches across the screen. An officer's legs, heels facing the camera, stand precariously on the muzzle. The stock of the sailor's rifle smashes against the officer's ankles. *(Cut to . . .)* — 551 / ECU **K53** *4*

(From below) The officer's feet, seen from front, slip backward off the cannon as the rifle swings away behind him. *(Cut to . . .)* — 552 / ECU **K54** *6*

The officer falls backward off the cannon. The leg of the sailor is cut by the frame. *(Cut to . . .)* — 553 / ECU **K55** *4*

A sailor holding a rifle stands balanced on a cannon barrel jutting out over the ocean. At its tip, an officer in dark jacket and white trousers falls backward and plummets head first toward the water below. *(Cut to . . .)* — 554 / LS **K56** *12*

The officer drops through the air toward the waves from the cannon high above. *(Cut to . . .)* — 555 / LS **K57** *6*

(From above) The ocean fills the frame. The officer hits the water with a great splash and disappears below the surface. *(Cut to . . .)* — 556 / LS **K58** *17*

(From the deck) The officer can barely be seen threshing about under the surface of the water. *(Cut to . . .)* — 557 / LS **K59** *36*

(Under water) The officer swims toward a tangle of weeds at the bottom. *(Cut to . . .)* — 558 / CU **K60** *73*

Dr. Smirnov crawls hurriedly into a hiding place on an upper — 559 / CU

554

559

deck. *(Cut to . . .)*   **N1**   *41*

As the surgeon tries to hide, a sailor approaches from above   560 / MS
him and another rushes him from the front. *(Cut to . . .)*   **N2**   *45*

The two sailors capture Dr. Smirnov in his hiding place. *(Cut* 561 / CU
to . . .)   **N3**   *26*

Struggling and protesting, the surgeon is hustled along the   562 / MS

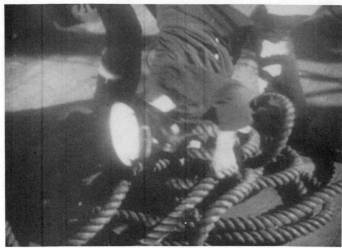

564

deck by the two sailors. *(Cut to . . .)* N4 *105*

The diminutive surgeon is held upside down by the two sailors. He clutches desperately at the heavy coils of a hawser beneath him on the deck. *(Cut to . . .)* 563 / CU N5 *67*

A third and a fourth sailor rush to the aid of the two holding the feet of the wriggling surgeon. *(Cut to . . .)* 564 / MS N6 *46*

The sailors try, unsuccessfully, to tear loose the surgeon's grasp on the hawser. The group staggers along the deck, dragging both the officer and the line. *(Cut to . . .)* 565 / CU N7 *46*

The sailors slowly haul away the dangling surgeon and the hawser. *(Cut to . . .)* 566 / MS N8 *26*

The hawser coils drag along the deck and out of the frame. A sailor's foot is seen in the background. *(Cut to . . .)* 567 / CU N9 *19*

The sailors carry the little surgeon feet first, like a carcass, up an iron stairway. *(Cut to . . .)* 568 / CU N10 *23*

The dangling surgeon gasps and protests feebly. His eyes are closed. His hands hang limp as he is carried slowly upward. *(Cut to . . .)* 569 / ECU N11 *17*

The priest lies crumpled at the bottom of the stairs where he 570 / ECU has fallen. One eye slowly, cautiously, opens for a moment, takes in the scene around him, then closes. He moves his head slightly to squint about, then quickly reassumes his sleeping position. *(Cut to . . .)*

J19   80

Dr. Smirnov's hand clutches feebly at the steps of the ladder up which he is being dragged. *(Cut to . . .)*

571 / ECU
N12   35

The legs of the sailors strain with the struggle of carrying the surgeon up the stairs. *(Cut to . . .)*

572 / ECU
N13   35

On the quarterdeck, a group of sailors runs toward the captain's companionway. They race down the steps. *(Cut to . . .)*

573 / MS
K61   43

(From above) A large group of armed sailors and Marines runs past the turret. *(Cut to . . .)*

574 / LS
K62   47

(From above) The sailors carrying the struggling Smirnov bring him to the edge of the deck near a lifeboat davit. *(Cut to . . .)*

575 / MS
N14   67

(From above) Two sailors struggle to get a better grip on the frantically twisting surgeon. In the background, the ocean

576 / LS
N15   40

578

fills the frame. *(Cut to . . .)*

(From above) The two sailors heave the surgeon's body into the air past the edge of the deck. *(Cut to . . .)*	577 /	MS
	N16	*20*

On the far side of the lifeboat davits, the two sailors sling the surgeon head first over the side of the vessel. His body falls out of the frame toward the water. *(Cut to . . .)*	578 /	MS
	N17	*12*

(From above) The surgeon falls toward the ocean below as the two sailors at the lifeboat station watch his plummeting descent. *(Cut to . . .)*	579 /	LS
	N18	*15*

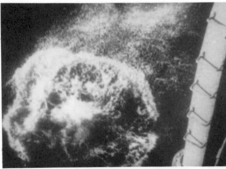

582

5

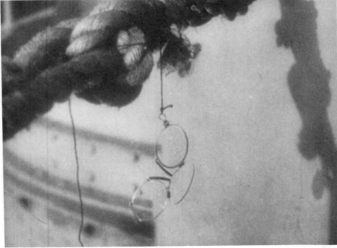

584

(From above) The surgeon's body drops swiftly toward the water. The spray of his splash explodes like a bomb as he hits the surface. *(Cut to . . .)*	580 / LS N19	23
(From above) From the lifeboat station three sailors watch the mushrooming spray of water. *(Cut to . . .)*	581 / LS N20	19
(From above) The spray created by the surgeon's body forms a foaming white circle on the surface of the ocean. *(Cut to . . .)*	582 / LS N21	18
Maggots crawl over the meat which the crew had refused to eat. *(Cut to . . .)*	583 / ECU O1	37
Down to Feed the Maggots *(Cut to . . .)*	TITLE	92
A thick hawser cuts across an upper corner of the frame. From it hangs the little surgeon's pince-nez, its ribbon tangled in the manila fibers. It swings gently back and forth, a symbol of Dr. Smirnov's blindness to the sailors' needs. *(Cut to . . .)*	584 / ECU N22	60
(From above) The quarterdeck of the *Potemkin* swarms with armed sailors. Individual officers are being surrounded and subdued. A dozen armed sailors run out on the turret top and wave to the crewmen below them. *(Cut to . . .)*	585 / LS K63	93
"Brothers! We've won!"	TITLE	93
(From above) The smoke of exuberantly fired rifles drifts across the crowded quarterdeck. The jubilant sailors wave their caps and shout joyously over their victory. *(Cut to . . .)*	586 / LS K64	48
The keyboard of the piano in the officers' salon is strewn with tattered sheet music. Broken candles and the crumpled candelabra are scattered over the scarred keys. *(Cut to . . .)*	587 / ECU M12	60
(From directly above) A deserted area of the upper deck, near the ventilators. After a few moments an officer runs across the area, pursued by three sailors. *(Cut to . . .)*	588 / LS L20	76

The brutal Gilyarovsky is after Vakulinchuk. *(Cut to . . .)* TITLE *134*

(From above) Gilyarovsky kneels on a perforated metal runway, rifle in hand. He peers offscreen intently, then leaps to his feet and rushes away. *(Cut to . . .)* 589 / CU
L21 *45*

Vakulinchuk climbs up on a gun mount, glances to the rear, then continues his escape. *(Cut to . . .)* 590 / MS
L22 *46*

Vakulinchuk clambers up a lifeboat girder and stands momentarily silhouetted against the sky. *(Cut to . . .)* 591 / MS
L23 *32*

As Vakulinchuk turns to determine Gilyarovsky's proximity, the officer steps out from behind a ventilator. The two study each other for a long moment. *(Cut to . . .)* 592 / MS
L24 *45*

Gilyarovsky stares in Vakulinchuk's direction. He raises his head, as if in triumph. *(Cut to . . .)* 593 / ECU
L25 *12*

598

(From below) Vakulinchuk stands on a lifeboat stanchion and waits tensely for the officer's next move. *(Cut to . . .)* — 594 / CU L26 22

Gilyarovsky's teeth are bared. He glances back hurriedly to see if anyone is coming. *(Cut to . . .)* — 595 / ECU L27 19

(From behind) Gilyarovsky holds his rifle pointed toward Vakulinchuk and turns for a moment to look behind him. Satisfied, he again faces the sailor and raises the rifle toward his shoulder. *(Cut to . . .)* — 596 / CU L28 19

Gilyarovsky sights along the barrel of the rifle. *(Cut to . . .)* — 597 / ECU L29 14

Gilyarovsky's face presses against the rifle stock. His finger slowly closes on the trigger. One eye opens wider and he strains to look rearward without moving his head. After a moment, he again takes aim at the sailor. *(Cut to . . .)* — 598 / ECU L30 26

Vakulinchuk, silhouetted against the sky, steps cautiously sideways on the lifeboat stanchion. *(Cut to . . .)* — 599 / MS L31 37

Rifle pressed against his face, Gilyarovsky aims at Vakulinchuk. *(Cut to . . .)* — 600 / ECU L32 9

Gilyarovsky's eye and nose fill the frame. Wisps of hair hang down across his face. His eye widens momentarily as he — 601 / ECU L33 9 shoots. *(Cut to . . .)*

Gilyarovsky fires. A puff of smoke floats from his rifle and obscures Vakulinchuk. *(Cut to . . .)*	602 **L34**	/	MS 6

(From below) Vakulinchuk, his back to the camera, lurches as he is hit. He clutches the back of his head and turns, staggering against a post for support. His hand drops. *(Cut to . . .)* 603 / CU **L35** *111*

Gilyarovsky watches intently, his rifle lowered. *(Cut to . . .)* 604 / CU **L36** *15*

Vakulinchuk pitches forward out of the frame. *(Cut to . . .)* 605 / CU **L37** *24*

The sailor falls from his perch and instinctively grasps at ropes hanging alongside the hull. His body swings out over the water. *(Cut to . . .)* 606 / MS **L38** *19*

For a moment Vakulinchuk clings to the ropes stretching downward. His strength ebbs and he plunges toward the water below. *(Cut to . . .)* 607 / LS **L39** *20*

(From directly above) A block and tackle hang above the water, held by ropes stretching upward out of the frame. Vakulinchuk's fall is broken by the large wooden block. He dangles there precariously, his arms clutching the ropes. *(Cut to . . .)* 608 / LS **L40** *31*

(From above) The quarterdeck of the *Potemkin* swarms with cheering, victorious sailors celebrating their successful revolt. *(Cut to . . .)* 609 / LS **K65** *24*

(From below) Silhouetted against the sky, a block and tackle hang from the outer end of a lifeboat davit. Six ropes run downward from it. *(Cut to . . .)* 610 / CU **L41** *5*

(From directly above) The block and tackle swing gently as Vakulinchuk feebly attempts to haul himself upright. *(Cut to . . .)* 611 / MS **L42** *49*

Beyond a dark doorway in the foreground, a boom stretches out over the water. The silhouetted figure of a sailor appears 612 / MS **L43** *29*

inside the doorway and looks out at the ocean. *(Cut to . . .)*

"Vakulinchuk is overboard!" *(Cut to . . .)*   TITLE   *125*

The silhouetted sailor in the doorway steps into the sunlight and runs out along the boom stretching over the water. Another sailor follows him through the doorway. *(Cut to . . .)*   613 / MS **L44** *59*

(From above) Three sailors run rapidly out on the boom, balancing themselves with the help of a running line. *(Cut to . . .)*   614 / MS **L45** *54*

(From above) The boom extends over the water below. Four sailors work their way out on it. *(Cut to . . .)*   615 / MS **L46** *44*

In the foreground, Vakulinchuk hangs suspended above the ocean on the block and tackle. Far beyond him, five sailors work their way out along a boom. *(Cut to . . .)*   616 / LS **L47** *65*

(From directly above) Vakulinchuk dangles head downward, his body wedged between the block and tackle. (Cut
to . . .)

| 617 | / | MS |
| **L48** | | 36 |

"Save Vakulinchuk!" (Cut to . . .)

| TITLE | 94 |

Eight sailors stand for a moment on the boom. Then they all
leap into the ocean to rescue the leader of their revolt. (Cut
to . . .)

| 618 | / | LS |
| **L49** | | 62 |

In the foreground, Vakulinchuk sags weakly on the block.
Behind him, the sailors hit the water and start swimming to
get under their wounded comrade before he falls. (Cut
to . . .)

| 619 | / | LS |
| **L50** | | 57 |

(From directly above) Vakulinchuk struggles to haul himself
to a sitting position with the aid of a hanging rope. The effort
exhausts him. He releases his grip and tumbles backward.
His body slips off the block and he falls head first into the
water below. (Cut to . . .)

| 620 | / | MS |
| **L51** | | 109 |

(From above) The sailors swiftly swim to the spot where Vakulinchuk disappeared. *(Cut to . . .)*   621 / LS
L52   *27*

Looking for Vakulinchuk, the sailors thresh about wildly in the water under the block. *(Fade out and cut to . . .)*   622 / MS
L53   *107*

(From above) Four crewmen slowly carry Vakulinchuk's body up an embarkation ladder which had been lowered to the water's edge. The rescue party is partly outside the frame, but its shadow rises along the *Potemkin*'s hull. At the top of the stairway the group halts with the dead man's bloody face in frame center. One of the sailors carrying Vakulinchuk's body wipes blood from the face with his hand and strokes the forehead tenderly. *(Iris in with slow fade and cut to . . .)*   623 / MS
L54   *327*

And he, who first raised the cry of revolt, was the first to fall at the hand of the executioner. *(Cut to . . .)*   TITLE   *206*

(From above) A launch enters the frame at bottom right and steams diagonally across the screen. A sailor stands at attention on the prow and an honor guard is lined up on either side of a low smokestack. Vakulinchuk's body, wrapped in a shroud, rests atop a cabin near the stern. Four sailors   624 / LS
P1   *328*

623

624

attend the dead hero. A black banner flutters from the flag-staff at the stern. *(Cut to . . .)*

To the Shore *(Cut to . . .)*   TITLE   *85*

(Irised view) A lighthouse guarding a harbor rises and falls with the horizon as if seen through a telescope aboard a rolling ship. The outer edges of the view are grey and diffused. *(Cut to . . .)*   625 / LS
                                                                 P2   *65*

Odessa *(Cut to . . .)*   TITLE   *85*

(From above) The funeral steam launch moves slowly across the screen from left to right. Black smoke trails rearward from its stack, while white steam sprays from nozzles at the waterline near the stern. The sailors attending Vakulinchuk's body stand stiffly at attention. The camera follows at a slower speed. *(Cut to . . .)*   626 / LS
                                                                 P3   *100*

(From above) The partially covered body of Vakulinchuk, half-hidden by white steam, rests on the cabin roof of the launch. An honor guard stands immobile at each corner. The camera moves with the launch. *(Cut to . . .)*   627 / LS
                                                                 P4   *90*

(From above) The small, dark silhouette of the launch moves across a glittering path of sunlight which partially illuminates a vast seascape. It leaves the sunny patch and   628 / LS
                                                                 P5   *106*

fades into the grey expanse beyond. *(Cut to . . .)*

(From above) The camera moves with the launch whose midship section extends across the frame. Vakulinchuk's body lies in state on the cabin roof. Steam and waves stream to the rear along both sides of the hull. *(Cut to . . .)*

629 / LS
P6 *101*

A tent on the new pier of Odessa was the last shelter of Vakulinchuk. *(Cut to . . .)*

TITLE *174*

A tent, silhouetted against the setting sun, stands on a pier. Beyond it, a tall, gaff-rigged schooner moves slowly across the water, its foresail gradually blocking the sun's rays. *(Cut to . . .)*

630 / LS
Q1 *108*

The body of Vakulinchuk, half in shadow, is stretched out on the pier. His clasped hands hold a burning candle on his

631 / CU
Q2 *37*

630

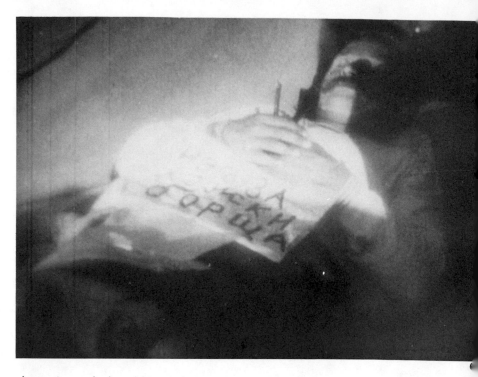

chest. A crude hand-lettered sign rests on his body. *(Cut to . . .)*

(Handlettered on paper) FOR A SPOONFUL OF SOUP *(Cut to . . .)*   TITLE   *83*

The candle in Vakulinchuk's hands fills the screen. Its flame flutters gently in the evening calm. *(Cut to . . .)*   632 / ECU **Q3**   *44*

Vakulinchuk's bare head and shoulders fill the screen as he lies in state on the pier. *(Cut to . . .)*   633 / ECU **Q4**   *70*

The dead sailor's heavy shoes extend from the loose shroud that covers his legs. *(Cut to . . .)*   634 / CU **Q5**   *35*

(From inside the tent) Darkness gradually envelops the pier. The tent flaps hang limply in the still air. Beyond, at the bottom of the screen, the candle flutters in Vakulinchuk's hands. In the distance, a sailing ship drifts slowly across the harbor as a dog trots past the tent. *(Cut to . . .)*   635 / LS **Q6**   *100*

It is twilight on the pier as the sun dips toward the horizon. A small harbor tug, barely visible, steams by. *(Cut to . . .)* 636 / LS
Q7 *127*

(From inside the tent) The dark of evening settles rapidly over the harbor. Only a few dancing rays of sunlight still dapple the waters beyond the pier. Shadows invade the tent, hiding the still body. *(Cut to . . .)* 637 / LS
Q8 *100*

Seen from the tent, the bowsprit of a large sailing vessel moves slowly in front of the setting sun. It gradually extinguishes the failing light and obliterates the outline of Vakulinchuk's body as it lies in state at the end of its journey. *(Quick fade out. Fade in to . . .)* 638 / LS
Q9 *273*

PART III
AN APPEAL FROM THE DEAD *(Fade out and cut to . . .)* TITLE *198*

(Irised view from the sea) A pale glow suffuses the night that envelops the dark, distant harbor. The seas are motionless, at rest. Broken clouds hang low over the city. *(Cut to . . .)* 639 / LS
A1 *41*

Night TITLE *78*

639

There is a hint of dawn. In the grey mist, a large sailing vessel rests quietly at anchor. Behind it, a large dockside crane slowly swings its load from ship to shore. *(Cut to . . .)*   640 / LS **A2** *216*

The sun looms behind the mists and burns a pale, flickering path of light across the harbor's waters. A tall sailing ship, deep in shadow, is anchored in the foreground. *(Cut to . . .)*   641 / LS **A3** *119*

The harbor is shrouded in early morning fog. A pair of three-masted sailing ships, their details dissolved in grey, rest quietly as they await the dawn. *(Cut to . . .)*   642 / LS **A4** *156*

A low, round buoy looms in the fog, a darker shape against the enveloping mist. Sea gulls huddle on its surface. *(Cut to . . .)*   643 / LS **A5** *94*

No wave breaks the oily calm of an empty stretch of sea. Down its center a growing path of light is barely perceptible. *(Cut to . . .)*   644 / LS **A6** *64*

The gull-covered buoy is now seen more clearly, its black hulk silhouetted against the increasing light. A gull soars off and flies away. *(Cut to . . .)*   645 / LS **A7** *31*

645

650

An empty sea stretches away, its horizon hidden in the mists. Soft light plays on its surface. *(Cut to . . .)*

646 / LS
A8 44

The bowsprit of a silhouetted sailing vessel at anchor juts diagonally across the scene. Far behind it, dockside cranes begin to appear in the dissolving early morning mists. *(Cut to . . .)*

647 / LS
A9 93

The camera moves slowly past steamships at dockside. In the clearing sky soft clouds appear. *(Cut to . . .)*

648 / LS
A10 114

The huge prow of a steamship at anchor slides past the moving camera. Its starboard side is clearly defined. The mists have lifted. *(Cut to . . .)*

649 / LS
A11 83

It is now dawn on the pier where Vakulinchuk lies. In the foreground, the candle in his crossed hands still burns. The black cloths on his tent flutter in the morning breeze. In the far distance, a sailboat lies at anchor. *(Cut to . . .)*

650 / LS
B1 46

The peak of Vakulinchuk's tent is silhouetted against the morning sky, adorned with black cloths. *(Cut to . . .)*

651 / CU
B2 54

The tent stands on a large, uncluttered pier. Its sides move in the morning breeze. An anchor and ring buoy rest nearby. Beyond, two men fish at the edge of the pier. A large vessel

652 / LS
B3 102

655

can be seen at its mooring. *(Cut to . . .)*

| The prow of a large steamship at anchor fills the screen. Heavy chains stretch downward from its bow toward the water. *(Cut to . . .)* | 653 / MS **A12** 35 |

The quay aroused curiosity. *(Cut to . . .)*   TITLE   *157*

| The tent on the pier begins to attract passersby. First a man, then two shawled women, and finally another man draw close to inspect the canvas shrine. *(Cut to . . .)* | 654 / LS **B4** 362 |

| *(From inside the tent)* People can be seen stopping to stare at the dead sailor who lies in the foreground. A mother and her two children stop and whisper to each other as they see the body. *(Cut to . . .)* | 655 / MS **B5** 114 |

| Vakulinchuk's shoulder and head fill the screen. The shadow of the tent falls across his face. *(Cut to . . .)* | 656 / CU **B6** 30 |

| *(From inside the tent)* More people are seen gathering in front of the body. As they watch, an old woman wearing a large kerchief over her head kneels at the dead sailor's side and trims the candle stuck in his hands. *(Cut to . . .)* | 657 / MS **B7** 287 |

| Two men fish off the side of the pier. They wait patiently for a nibble on their lines. Even the cat between them barely | 658 / MS **B8** 100 |

moves. *(Cut to . . .)*

The candle in Vakulinchuk's hands fills the screen. Its flame wavers gently. *(Cut to . . .)*	659 / ECU **B9** 33
Half in the tent's shadow, the sailor's white-uniformed body lies on the pier. *(Cut to . . .)*	660 / CU **B10** 50
(From inside the tent) Two poorly dressed working women kneel at Vakulinchuk's feet in contemplation of the body and its sign, "For a spoonful of soup." The pier behind them is now filled with silent figures. Occasionally other spectators pause at the tent opening. Though their heads are cut by the frame, their clothes reveal their class. Two workers doff their caps; a white-bloused middle-class woman with straw hat looks in; even a richly dressed woman carrying a white parasol pauses briefly to observe the sailor. *(Cut to . . .)*	661 / MS **B11** 513
The foresail of a moored sailing ship is slowly lowered. *(Cut to . . .)*	662 / MS **A13** 49
Along with the sun, rose the whole city! *(Cut to . . .)*	TITLE 134
The screen is evenly divided into three vertical panels. The right and left panels are black. In the center panel, a long, narrow, empty staircase runs up the side of a steep hill from the bottom of the screen. Five terraces break the infinity of rising steps. Suddenly, in a dissolve, the empty steps are thronged with the people of Odessa descending briskly. *(Cut to . . .)*	663 / LS **C1** 130
The right and left panels of the screen are black. In the center panel, the leading citizens are now closer to the camera. Behind them, the entire stairway is covered with people. *(Cut to . . .)*	664 / LS **C2** 62
The Battleship at Anchorage *(Cut to . . .)*	TITLE 126
The descending stairway crosses the frame diagonally. The individuals on it can now be distinguished. They are mostly workers and women wearing kerchiefs. *(Cut to . . .)*	665 / MS **C3** 60

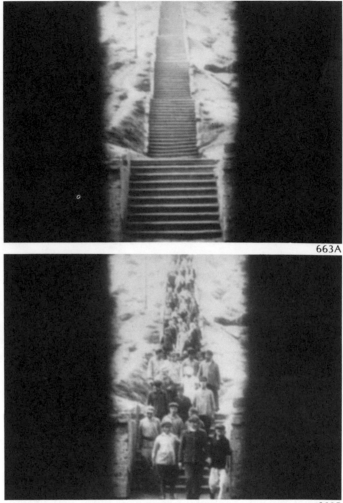

663A

663B

A never-ending swarm of civilians descends the steps, which extend diagonally downward across the entire hillside. At the bottom of the stairs, the throng moves purposefully along a road and offscreen. *(Cut to . . .)*	666 **C4**	/	LS *51*
. . . uprising . . . *(Cut to . . .)*	TITLE		*85*
The column of people moves along a road bordering a nar-	667	/	LS

row stream and then turns, crossing a low bridge to the other bank. *(Cut to . . .)* **C5** *65*

The bridge across the stream spans the screen left to right. The massed file of people moves quietly but steadily behind its low parapet. *(Cut to . . .)* 668 / **C6** MS *64*

Near an embankment, the crowd pushes steadily across the screen as if each individual is being drawn forward by a magnet. In the foreground, wash on a line dries in the sun. In the far background, a vast aqueduct is seen dimly. *(Cut to . . .)* 669 / **C7** LS *102*

. . . the shore . . . *(Cut to . . .)* TITLE *94*

(From above) The crowd fans out across a pier, moving past the dark hull of a steamship moored alongside. *(Cut to . . .)* 670 / **C8** LS *103*

. . . a dead sailor . . . *(Cut to . . .)* TITLE *123*

(From above) The citizens of Odessa file past the tent before which lies the body of Vakulinchuk. The men have bared 671 / **B12** MS *132*

666

their heads in respect for the dead. A couple pauses for a moment to place a coin on a barrel outside the tent. Two women in black stand near the body. *(Cut to . . .)*

A young boy stands at the entrance to the tent, staring at the dead sailor. He drops a coin into Vakulinchuk's hat on the barrel. *(Cut to . . .)*	672 / **B13**	CU *62*
The morning sun illuminates the sign and the candle in Vakulinchuk's folded hands as he lies on the pier. *(Cut to . . .)*	673 / **B14**	CU *54*
A hand adds a coin to the growing pile in the sailor's hat on the barrel head. *(Cut to . . .)*	674 / **B15**	ECU *29*
People of all classes move soberly past the tent—kerchiefed peasant women, working men, elegant ladies with parasols. *(Cut to . . .)*	675 / **B16**	MS *67*
The crowd moves up a short flight of stairs at the edge of the pier to reach the tent. In the background, a long, narrow	676 / **B17**	MS *104*

676

678

jetty curves away into the distance, jammed with curious citizens. *(Cut to . . .)*

Seen from the upper deck of a moored vessel, the people of Odessa move along the distant jetty in a long file, cut by the frame top. *(Cut to . . .)* 677 / LS **B18** *98*

(From high above) The camera looks down at the mass of 678 / LS

citizens who surround Vakulinchuk's tent. After a moment, it slowly pans back along the narrow breakwater leading to the pier. The full length of the enormous breakwater comes into view. As far as the eye can see it is black with an endless column of people who press forward to view the body. *(Cut to . . .)*   **B19** *430*

In the city, citizens on their way to the pier descend a curving, balustraded stairway that leads under the arches of a great viaduct. *(Cut to . . .)*   679 / LS **C9** *124*

(From high above) The camera slowly pans from the waves of people crowding the length of the immense breakwater to the endless waves of the harbor waters. *(Cut to . . .)*   680 / LS **C10** *133*

At the base of the great viaduct, the curving stairways on either side discharge their human streams into a broad river of curious, sympathetic people that flows steadily down toward the harbor. *(Cut to . . .)*   681 / LS **C11** *100*

Under the vaulting black arch of the great viaduct, the human tide fills the screen from side to side—a vast reaching out of Odessa's heart toward the dead sailor on the pier. *(Cut to . . .)*   682 / LS **C12** *63*

682

(From directly above) An enormous ring of people jammed tightly together on the pier surrounds the sailor's tent. It fills the screen to its edges. *(Cut to . . .)*

683 / LS
B20 *106*

(From above) At the entrance to Vakulinchuk's tent, two

684 / LS

683

684

figures stand out from the crowd—a smartly dressed woman in white with straw hat and white parasol and a dark woman in black who addresses the citizens near her. *(Cut to . . .)*	**D1**	53
"We will remember!" *(Cut to . . .)*	TITLE	110
The woman in black speaks intensely to those around the tent, facing them and emphasizing her words with quick gestures. She turns and points to the body. *(Cut to . . .)*	685 / **D2**	MS 35
(Hand-lettered on paper) FOR A SPOONFUL OF SOUP *(Cut to . . .)*	TITLE	75
The woman in black continues to address the crowd from in front of the tent. *(Cut to . . .)*	686 / **D3**	MS 66
"For a spoonful of soup!"	TITLE	109
A young sailor on the pier declaims passionately from a paper in his hand. His clenched fist emphasizes each phrase. Behind him, citizens move past. *(Cut to . . .)*	687 / **D4**	CU 73

"People of Odessa!
    Before you lies the body of Grigori Vakulinchuk, a sailor cruelly murdered by the senior officer of the battleship *Potemkin*. We will avenge ourselves! Death to the oppressors!
        The Crew of the *Potemkin*" *(Cut to . . .)*
	TITLE	505

The youthful sailor continues reading loudly and with deep feeling the message from the *Potemkin*'s crew. Behind him a worker stops to listen. *(Cut to . . .)*	688 / **D5**	CU 46
Two black-shawled peasant women bow their heads in grief. *(Cut to . . .)*	689 / **B21**	CU 83
An old peasant woman kneeling at Vakulinchuk's side bends over and kisses his hand. Onlookers move by behind them. *(Cut to . . .)*	690 / **B22**	CU 130
Vakulinchuk's face, half in shadow, fills the screen. *(Cut to . . .)*	691 / **B23**	ECU 18
An ancient, grey-haired woman clasps her handkerchief and	692 /	CU

sobs. *(Cut to . . .)*	**B24**	*75*
A white-bearded, professorial figure wearing a fine coat removes his pince-nez in deep emotion as he looks down at the body. *(Cut to . . .)*	693 / **B25**	CU *48*
Two women, seen from the waist down, stand at the dead sailor's feet. They drop to their knees and bend to touch his legs with their heads. *(Cut to . . .)*	694 / **B26**	CU *36*
A sharp-faced man wearing a jaunty straw hat smiles cynically at the scene he is observing and coolly draws on his cigarette. He looks away with an amused expression as he exhales. *(Cut to . . .)*	695 / **E1**	CU *62*
The top of a woman's bowed head fills the lower half of the screen. It moves as she sobs. *(Cut to . . .)*	696 / **B27**	ECU *27*
Eternal memory for the fallen fighters! *(Cut to . . .)*	TITLE	*110*
On the pier three simply dressed women sing with mournful expressions. *(Cut to . . .)*	697 / **B28**	MS *51*
All for one . . . *(Cut to . . .)*	TITLE	*73*
Four vigorous young workers join the lament for the fallen sailor. *(Cut to . . .)*	698 / **B29**	CU *64*
. . . one . . . *(Cut to . . .)*	TITLE	*54*
Vakulinchuk's head and shoulders, seen from the side, fill the frame. Shadows move over his face. *(Cut to . . .)*	699 / **B30**	ECU *36*
. . . for all. *(Cut to . . .)*	TITLE	*102*
(From directly overhead) The vast throng around the tent on the pier trembles as if everyone is singing with intense fervor for the dead sailor. *(Cut to . . .)*	700 / **B31**	LS *44*
Two working women, one with eyes closed, sing sadly. *(Cut to . . .)*	701 / **B32**	CU *47*
An old woman with deeply lined face wipes a tear from her eye and sobs. In the background, people move past her. *(Cut to . . .)*	702 / **B33**	ECU *99*

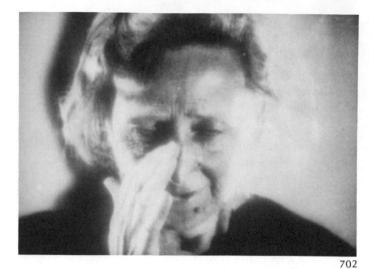

702

A mother stands with her son, father, and husband in sorrowful silence. *(Cut to . . .)*

703 / CU
B34 *88*

Three workers stare downward grimly. After a moment, the two in front remove their caps. The third hesitates slightly. Then he, too, shows his respect for the dead sailor. *(Cut to . . .)*

704 / CU
B35 *57*

704

The old woman with the handkerchief wipes her eyes and presses a hand to her forehead in deep emotion. *(Cut to . . .)*

705 / CU
B36 54

(From above) The accusing placard placed on Vakulin-chuk's body fills the screen. *(Cut to . . .)*

706 / ECU
B37 49

(From directly overhead) A great throng of people is massed around the tent, drawn by the mute evidence of murderous Czarist brutality. *(Cut to . . .)*

707 / LS
B38 26

Three workers stare downward soberly. They neither move nor speak. *(Cut to . . .)*

708 / CU
B39 49

A bearded hod carrier wearing a burlap sack over his head and shoulders watches with heavy heart. He sighs deeply, raises a rough hand to his brow and bows his head in grief. *(Cut to . . .)*

709 / CU
B40 140

Two hands nervously hold a neat black cap, squeezing and twisting it under emotional strain. *(Cut to . . .)*

710 / CU
B41 42

The bearded hod carrier stands with a calloused, stiff hand pressed against the brow of his bowed head. *(Cut to . . .)*

711 / CU
B42 39

712

Suddenly, the gathering storm of emotion finds an outlet in the crowd massed around the tent. An agitator with fiery voice and blazing eyes stands on a stump and shouts to the people whose faces are turned toward him. *(Cut to . . .)*	712 / **D6**	CU 49
"Down with the executioners!"	TITLE	*101*
The head of a young man, seen from the side and rear, fills the screen. He is listening intently to the speaker. *(Cut to . . .)*	713 / **D7**	ECU *11*
Two smocked peasants with grizzled grey hair, their backs to the camera, stare in the direction of the agitator. *(Cut to . . .)*	714 / **D8**	CU *21*
A hand angrily grips a jacket bottom, then slowly forms a tight fist in response to the agitator's inflammatory words. *(Cut to . . .)*	715 / **D9**	ECU *30*
Two workers, seen from the rear and side, look intently offscreen. *(Cut to . . .)*	716 / **D10**	CU *9*
The two smocked peasants, seen from the rear, stare toward the agitator. *(Cut to . . .)*	717 / **D11**	CU *6*
The two workers still stare offscreen. *(Cut to . . .)*	718 / **D12**	CU *6*
A listener's clenched fist slowly rises from waist level. *(Cut to . . .)*	719 / **D13**	ECU *10*
The fist, seen from the front, seems poised to strike. *(Cut to . . .)*	720 / **D14**	ECU *13*
The faces of angry workers and peasants crowd the screen, vigorously shouting their support to the agitator. *(Cut to . . .)*	721 / **D15**	CU *35*
Another agitator, a black-haired woman in dark jacket, now incites the crowd. She stands on a stump and exhorts the people around her. *(Cut to . . .)*	722 / **D16**	CU *38*
A hand held like a claw, fingers tensely curved, slowly closes in growing rage. *(Cut to . . .)*	723 / **D17**	ECU *28*

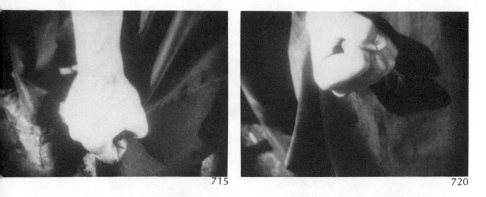

715 720

The female agitator continues to arouse the crowd, her hand flailing the air to emphasize her words. *(Cut to . . .)* 724 / CU **D18** *17*

The old woman who had been wiping her eyes with a handkerchief now throws her head back. She inhales deeply as if to prepare for some crucial act, swings her arm wide and cries out. *(Cut to . . .)* 725 / CU **D19** *46*

The passionately clenched fist leaps from a listener's side forward out of the frame. *(Cut to . . .)* 726 / ECU **D20** *108*

The screen bristles with a forest of fists raised and shaking in demand for action against the callous slayers of the dead 727 / CU **D21** *71*

722

727

728

sailor. *(Cut to . . .)*

A group of women in the crowd echo the men's violent outburst. They shout, shake their fists; one whips off her fine straw hat and waves it excitedly. *(Cut to . . .)*	728 / CU **D22** 40

The old woman cries out in rapturous affirmation. *(Cut to . . .)*	729 / CU **D23** 24

The workers and peasants continue to shout approval of the agitator's demands. Their gestures and cries erupt volcanically. *(Cut to . . .)*	730 / CU **D24** 60

The female agitator continues to harangue the crowd. *(Cut to . . .)*	731 / CU **D25** 20

The group of women cry out their agreement. The woman with the straw hat turns to those behind her. She waves the hat high above her head. *(Cut to . . .)*	732 / CU **D26** 26

The group of shouting workers and peasants begins to surge forward. *(Cut to . . .)*	733 / CU **D27** 32

The group of women become violently agitated. They shake their fists with the fury of their feelings. *(Cut to . . .)*	734 / CU **D28** 27

Not everyone is caught up in the emotional storm at the sailor's bier. Facing the camera, two well-dressed men observe the tumult. One wears a straw hat, vest, and wing collar. With thumbs hooked in his vest, he waves his fingers deprecatingly. An amused sneer at the crowd's disorderly behavior covers his face as he looks at his neighbors on either side. The men behind him stand expectantly still. *(Cut to . . .)*	735 / CU **E2** 75

The group of women wildly wave their arms. *(Cut to . . .)*	736 / CU **D29** 21

"Mothers and brothers! Let there be no difference or enmity between us!" *(Cut to . . .)*	TITLE 174

The women continue their highly-charged outburst. *(Cut to . . .)*	737 / CU **D30** 28

735

The sneering face of the well-dressed man fills the screen. The wild outcries of the aroused citizens evoke his amused ridicule. *(Cut to . . .)*	738 / E3	ECU 27

The female agitator turns from haranguing the crowd to comment harshly on the attitude of the well-dressed citizen. *(Cut to . . .)*	739 / E4	CU 26

The scoffer laughs derisively. An angry look flashes momentarily over his face as he speaks. *(Cut to . . .)*	740 / E5	ECU 20

"Down with the Jews!" *(Cut to . . .)*	TITLE	94

The face of the well-dressed onlooker breaks into a smirking grin. He is enjoying his success at twisting the agitator's demand for justice against the executioners. *(Cut to . . .)*	741 / E6	ECU 15

A mariner facing away from the camera suddenly turns and moves forward until his face fills the screen. He glares with terrible hate; his features are livid with rage. *(Cut to . . .)*	742 / E7	ECU 8

The mariner, now slightly farther away, mutters an oath. His face and shoulders fill the screen. *(Cut to . . .)*	743 / E8	CU 10

The two grizzled peasants seen earlier turn around to stare menacingly at the offscreen mocker. *(Cut to . . .)*	744 / E9	CU 10

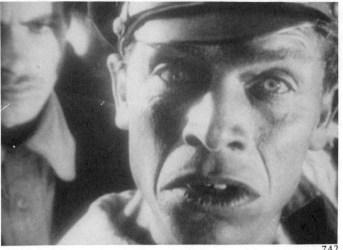

742

Two workers also turn around to stare with blazing eyes at the well-dressed onlooker offscreen. *(Cut to . . .)*	745 / **E10**	CU 27
The snickering observer shakes his head with pleasure at his own wit. *(Cut to . . .)*	746 / **E11**	ECU 29
The dark, savage face of the mariner contorts with a snarling threat. *(Cut to . . .)*	747 / **E12**	ECU 9
The smile fades abruptly from the face of the scoffer. His eyes widen. He is startled by the intensity of the outburst directed at him. *(Cut to . . .)*	748 / **E13**	ECU 13
The mariner lunges forward. The upper half of his contorted face fills the screen. *(Cut to . . .)*	749 / **E14**	ECU 16
The startled onlooker instinctively steps back from the threatening outburst. He pulls the large brim of his hat down over his eyes, turns up the collar of his white linen jacket and attempts to slink away. At the first step, a neighbor's hand clamps down on his shoulder to stop him. *(Cut to . . .)*	750 / **E15**	CU 42
The two workers speak sharply to the offscreen mocker. *(Cut to . . .)*	751 / **E16**	CU 17
The onlooker is yanked backward roughly by the hand grasping his shoulder. *(Cut to . . .)*	752 / **E17**	CU 9

(From above) He is jostled by the closely-packed group around him and his hat is knocked off. *(Cut to . . .)*

753 / MS
E18 *12*

The attacked man sways off-balance as he is pushed backward. He gasps open-mouthed. A fist is raised. Other heads blot his from view. *(Cut to . . .)*

754 / CU
E19 *24*

(From above) The scoffer is beset by the pushing crowd around him. His mouth is open wide in surprise and

755 / MS
E20 *33*

pain. The crowd closes over him as he sinks beneath their blows. *(Cut to . . .)*

A blur of backs and slashing arms fills the screen. *(Cut to . . .)* 756 / ECU **E21** *12*

The agitator speaks passionately to the crowd around him. He tears at his hair, flings his arms wide in fury. *(Cut to . . .)* 757 / CU **D31** *43*

The two workers, aroused by the agitator, cry out to each other and exchange impassioned declarations. *(Cut to . . .)* 758 / CU **D32** *61*

An older worker, determined to fight for justice, raises his fists. His grim face fills the screen. *(Cut to . . .)* 759 / ECU **D33** *13*

The group of women led by the well-dressed woman with the fine straw hat shouts a fiery demand for action. *(Cut to . . .)* 760 / CU **D34** *42*

The agitator responds to their approval with further goading. *(Cut to . . .)* 761 / CU **D35** *15*

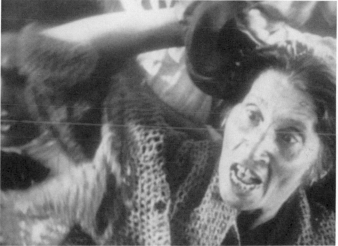

762

A black-shawled peasant woman is beside herself with excitement. Her lean, dark face is distorted as she shouts to those around her. In a paroxysm of emotion, she rips the shawl from her head and swings it about her like a torch. *(Cut to . . .)*

762 / CU
D36   *80*

The agitator, speaking passionately, slashes the air with his cap. *(Cut to . . .)*

763 / CU
D37   *19*

The peasant woman is in the grip of an uncontrollable frenzy. She screams, flails about her with her shawl, twists and turns. At her side, the well-dressed young woman shares her fiery outburst. *(Cut to . . .)*

764 / CU
D38   *68*

The agitator continues to feed the fire he has kindled among his listeners. He cries out, pointing dramatically with his arm. *(Cut to . . .)*

765 / CU
D39   *62*

"Shoulder to shoulder!" *(Cut to . . .)*

TITLE   *94*

In Odessa, a vast outpouring of people advance shoulder to shoulder down two great stairways and under the giant arch of an enormous viaduct. *(Cut to . . .)*

766 / LS
C13   *59*

765

766

The land—for us!	TITLE	*80*
The human tide flows under an immense stone arch. *(Cut to . . .)*	767 / **C14**	LS *111*
Tomorrow—for us!	TITLE	*94*
The camera is now farther from the arch and includes a wider scene. The stone arch is one of many giant spans of a colossal viaduct. Two streams of people traverse it—one moving along the top, the other passing under the arch far below. *(Cut to . . .)*	768 / **C15**	LS *119*
The peasant woman, her back to the camera, and the young well-dressed woman are carried away by their frenzied indignation over the slaying of Vakulinchuk. They shout, swing their arms about their heads, cry out in rage. *(Cut to . . .)*	769 / **D40**	CU *37*
The raised arms of men in the crowd shaking their clenched fists fill the screen. *(Cut to . . .)*	770 / **D41**	CU *17*
The agitator continues his incandescent attack on the crowd's emotions. *(Cut to . . .)*	771 / **D42**	CU *63*
A young man rips his shirt in frenzied response to the agitator. *(Cut to . . .)*	772 / **D43**	CU *17*

774

775

The well-dressed young woman whirls about to face the crowd, as if calling them to follow. *(Cut to . . .)* 773 / CU **D44** *25*

The storm of raised fists fills the screen. *(Cut to . . .)* 774 / CU **D45** *20*

(From above) On the quarterdeck of the battleship *Potemkin* a wave of sailors runs abruptly from under the shelter 775 / LS **F1** *57*

of the gun turret and scatters across the deck. *(Cut to . . .)*

The bridge of the *Potemkin* is overrun by sailors at every level. *(Cut to . . .)*	776 / F2	LS 67
The bridge and gun turret, seen from the side, swarm with the mutineers who have captured control of the ship from its officers. *(Cut to . . .)*	777 / F3	LS 52
In a closer, head-on view, the *Potemkin*'s bridge and control turret are deluged with sailors. *(Cut to . . .)*	778 / F4	LS 23
A Delegate from the Shore *(Cut to . . .)*	TITLE	102
(From below) A civilian appears among the sailors on the ship's bridge and addresses the assembled crew. *(Cut to . . .)*	779 / F5	MS 54
"The enemy has been dealt a decisive blow!" *(Cut to . . .)*	TITLE	102
The civilian and a sailor stand on the bridge, their backs to the camera, addressing the crew on the teeming quarterdeck below. The civilian emissary is exultant. He waves his arm triumphantly. *(Cut to . . .)*	780 / F6	CU 58
"Together with the rising workers of all Russia . . ." *(Cut to . . .)*	TITLE	133
(From below) The emissary proclaims his mission to the sailors crowding around the bridge of the *Potemkin*. *(Cut to . . .)*	781 / F7	MS 57
(From above) The quarterdeck is closely packed with sailors looking up at the bridge. *(Cut to . . .)*	782 / F8	LS 37
"We will win!" *(Cut to . . .)*	TITLE	77
The sailors swarming around the bridge raise their white caps in a cheer. *(Cut to . . .)*	783 / F9	MS 35
(From below) Caps wave and the emissary raises his arms exultantly as the crew applauds the support of the people of Odessa. *(Cut to . . .)*	784 / F10	LS 41

(From the side) The bridge and the turret of the battleship are alive with caps waving in triumph. *(Cut to . . .)*   785 / LS
F11   *14*

(From below) The muzzles of the *Potemkin*'s two forward guns loom up boldly at the bottom of the screen, framing the ecstatic seamen behind them on the bridge and the control tower. *(Cut to . . .)*   786 / LS
F12   *29*

The emissary on the bridge, his back to the camera, continues to pledge the sympathy and support of the city. *(Cut to . . .)*   787 / CU
F13   *32*

(From below) The crow's nest of the *Potemkin* is jammed with cheering sailors. *(Cut to . . .)*   788 / LS
F14   *23*

Tensely and vigilantly the shore watched over the *Potemkin. (Cut to . . .)*   TITLE   *48*

Crowding the steps of a vast stairway leading down to the harbor, a huge multitude of Odessa's citizens stand anx-   789 / LS
G1   *71*

iously looking out over the water. White parasols shade some from the sun. In a few places, children squat on the stairs. *(Cut to . . .)*

(A closer view) In the forefront of the throng that covers the immense stairway stands a well-dressed group of adults and children. *(Cut to . . .)*   790 / LS — **G2** 54

(From above) On the quarterdeck of the *Potemkin,* the assembled sailors gaze upward. *(Cut to . . .)*   791 / LS — **F15** 39

(From above) Three sailors wave their hands excitedly and point upward. Behind them, other sailors on the quarterdeck watch intently. *(Cut to . . .)*   792 / MS — **F16** 61

(From below) A sailor stands at the crow's nest of the ship, on the highest crossbar of the mast. Rising into the frame   793 / LS — **F17** 88

789

from the bottom of the screen, a huge flag is hoisted into place behind him. *(Cut to . . .)*

(From above) Two sailors wave their caps excitedly as they look up. Beyond them, surrounding the giant cannon on the quarterdeck, other sailors cheer the flag's hoisting. *(Cut to . . .)*

794 / MS
F18 44

The throng of intently watching civilians standing on the Odessa steps suddenly comes to life as the flag goes up. Hands, hats, and handkerchiefs wave cheerfully; parasols bob. *(Cut to . . .)*

795 / LS
G3 48

(From below) At the peak of the *Potemkin*'s mast, a large forked flag waves triumphantly in the wind, a symbol of successful revolt. *(Cut and fade in to . . .)*

796 / LS
F19 37

PART IV
THE ODESSA STEPS *(Fade out and fade in to . . .)*

TITLE 213

That memorable day the city lived one life with the rebellious battleship. *(Cut to . . .)*

TITLE 191

797

The foreground is crisscrossed with the masts and furled sails of more than a dozen sailboats drawn up along the shore in the Odessa harbor. After a moment, sailors clamber aboard quickly and start casting off. *(Cut to . . .)*	797 / **A1**	LS *118*
White-winged boats flew to the *Potemkin. (Cut to . . .)*	TITLE	*109*
As the sailboats get under way across the harbor, five citizens carrying packages walk along a gangplank toward a boat moored at the water's edge. *(Cut to . . .)*	798 / **A2**	LS *96*
A large white sail fills the screen. At the prow, a sailor pushes the boat off from the shore. As the sail glides to the right out of the frame, it reveals the waters beyond, crowded with hurrying craft. *(Cut to . . .)*	799 / **A3**	MS *114*
The citizens on the gangplank climb aboard the waiting boat. The fluttering white wings of a fowl and a heaped basket reveal the citizens' mission. They are carrying food	800 / **A4**	MS *108*

to the mutinying sailors of the *Potemkin. (Cut to . . .)*

Boats hoisting sail for the visit to the ship crowd the screen. *(Cut to . . .)*	801 / **A5**	MS *85*

The harbor is alive with a squadron of boats sailing smoothly, swiftly across the water, parallel to the horizontals of the frame. Their sails form crescent-shaped triangles of alternating dark and light. *(Cut to . . .)* — 802 / **A6** — LS *134*

(From above) The squadron of speeding yawls moves evenly across the screen from upper left to lower right. *(Cut to . . .)* — 803 / **A7** — LS *101*

Swiftly moving yawls are seen in the far distance beyond five tall stone columns which rise from a stone balustrade on shore. The balustrade forms a dark arch that contrasts sharply with the horizontal movement of the boats. *(Cut to . . .)* — 804 / **A8** — LS *143*

A stream of people moves rapidly under a huge shadowed arch, on its way to watch the departing yawls. Far beyond, the crescent tips of white sails move slowly across the harbor. *(Cut to . . .)* — 805 / **B1** — LS *126*

Two watchers on shore reflect the offscreen passage of the sailing fleet in the movement of their eyes. The man is bearded, dressed in sober city clothes. The woman wears a white blouse and a wide-brimmed straw hat. She carries a dark parasol. *(Cut to . . .)* — 806 / **B2** — CU *72*

Two men in dark fatigue jackets stand on either side of a thin-faced woman wearing a light-colored blouse. They happily observe the progress of the offscreen squadron. *(Cut to . . .)* — 807 / **B3** — CU *15*

The bearded man and the white-bloused woman with parasol wave enthusiastically toward the yawls. *(Cut to . . .)* — 808 / **B4** — CU *67*

A mature, refined woman, her arm around the shoulders of a young girl, watches the offscreen fleet and nods approvingly. The woman wears pince-nez. Her small black hat is held in place with a white scarf tied under her chin. She has — 809 / **C1** — CU *68*

805

809

been seen previously among the citizens standing on the vast steps. *(Cut to . . .)*

A bespectacled young student in a white sweater peers toward the harbor with his hand to his brow to deflect the sun's glare. He raises his hand, waves, and begins to cheer the yawls. *(Cut to . . .)*

810 / ECU
B5 *35*

(From a yawl) Over the open sea a large sloop sails swiftly

811 / LS

into view from the right. It overtakes the moving camera,   **A9**   *68*
sailing out of the frame on the left. *(Cut to . . .)*

From the deck of one of the speeding yawls, we look aft and   812 / LS
see a vast armada under sail, all moving swiftly toward the   **A10**   *149*
Potemkin. (Cut to . . .)

On the deck of the battleship, sailors rush to the rail and   813 / MS

wildly greet the distant boats as they approach. *(Cut to . . .)*   **D1**   *58*

One of the sailboats slowly overtakes the camera. As it passes nearby from right to left its great gaff-rigged sail fills the screen momentarily, hiding the many craft that dot the harbor behind it. *(Cut to . . .)*   814 / MS   **A11** *165*

The *Potemkin*'s shipside ladder leads down to the water's edge where many yawls have tied up at the landing platform. A crewman hurries down the steps toward the boats, moving out of the frame. *(Cut to . . .)*   815 / CU   **D2** *54*

From directly aft, two yawls overtake the moving camera and sail past on a long, curving tack. *(Cut to . . .)*   816 / LS   **A12** *136*

Above the looming hull of the *Potemkin,* seen from the water, sailors crowd the rails and turret, waving and cheering. Below, the tips of sails cut by the bottom frame glide by. *(Cut to . . .)*   817 / LS   **A13** *67*

A heavily laden sailboat maneuvers past the hull of the *Potemkin,* which towers beyond it. *(Cut to . . .)*   818 / MS   **A14** *20*

At a gun turret on the deck of the *Potemkin,* a half-dozen sailors stand and wave to the boats seen in the distance. A larger group hurries into the scene to join them in the welcome. *(Cut to . . .)*   819 / MS   **D3** *76*

The side of the *Potemkin* is seen from the water. Sailors at the rail wave as an ever-growing number of sailboats go gliding by. Only the tops of the sails are seen above the bottom frame. *(Cut to . . .)*   820 / LS   **A15** *77*

On the deck of the *Potemkin* sailors begin descending the shipside ladder. *(Cut to . . .)*   821 / MS   **D4** *69*

A sailboat and a rowboat move in toward the *Potemkin*'s hull. *(Cut to . . .)*   822 / LS   **A16** *75*

Beyond a deckrail of the *Potemkin,* the succoring sailboats gathered below at its landing platform can be seen lowering   823 / LS   **D5** *75* their sails. A sailor waves from one of the boats. *(Cut to . . .)*

A giant cannon of the *Potemkin* stretches out over the sea. Below, the sharp peaks of the sails on the moored boats begin to lower. *(Cut to . . .)*   824 / LS **D6** 91

The empty deckrail of the *Potemkin,* which overlooks the moored boats huddled below, is suddenly crowded with sailors who rush into the frame to wave to the boatmen. *(Cut to . . .)*   825 / LS **D7** 70

A curving deckrail of the *Potemkin* cuts across the lower right-hand corner of the frame. Far below on the water, sailboats and rowboats fill the screen as they gather with their cargoes of gifts. *(Cut to . . .)*   826 / LS **D8** 97

On a lower deck of the *Potemkin,* two sailors waiting at the   827 / MS

rail converse eagerly with the newly arrived boatmen, who are lowering their sails. *(Cut to . . .)*   **D9**   *97*

In one of the yawls, a boatman displays a package he has brought the *Potemkin*'s sailors, while his partner lowers sail. *(Cut to . . .)*   828 / MS   **A17**   *59*

Other sailors hurry to the battleship's rail to wave to the boats below. The screen is crowded with the arching backs of the sailors as they lean forward eagerly. *(Cut to . . .)*   829 / MS   **D10**   *41*

The multitude of watching citizens on the Odessa steps wave their arms in a great cheer as contact is made offscreen between the succoring squadron and the battleship. *(Cut to . . .)*   830 / LS   **B6**   *53*

A sailor at the top of the shipside ladder extends his arms as the first civilian, a woman, comes up toward him. She carries a gift, a live, wing-flapping goose. *(Cut to . . .)*   831 / MS   **D11**   *88*

The boatmen in the yawls moored at the foot of the *Potemkin*'s embarking ladder form a package-passing chain, throwing the gifts from boat to boat. *(Cut to . . .)*   832 / MS   **A18**   *74*

A closer view of the cheering, waving throng on the Odessa   833 / LS

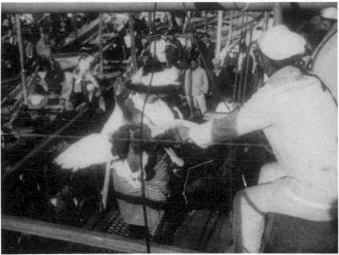

831

steps. In the immediate foreground stands a group of men, women and children. One of them, a woman wearing pince-nez, and a young girl were previously seen in closeup. *(Cut to . . .)*	**B7**	46
The gathered yawls, seen from a rail of the *Potemkin,* bustle with passengers picking their way toward the battleship. *(Cut to . . .)*	834 / **D12**	LS *81*
The top of the shipside ladder is crowded with arriving civilians and sailors. Packages change hands. A live pig is handed to one of the crewmen. *(Cut to . . .)*	835 / **D13**	MS *97*
A group of sailors happily lifts a large crate of live fowl aboard. *(Cut to . . .)*	836 / **D14**	CU *64*
A civilian on deck gives a live goose to someone offscreen. *(Cut to . . .)*	837 / **D15**	CU *20*
Civilians and crewmen embrace fraternally on deck. *(Cut to . . .)*	838 / **D16**	CU *55*
A large basket filled with fresh eggs is brought aboard by a civilian and presented to a crewman. *(Cut to . . .)*	839 / **D17**	CU *43*
At the crowded shipside ladder, a woman hands another live pig to a waiting crewman. *(Cut to . . .)*	840 / **D18**	MS *44*
The large throng on the Odessa steps watches the offscreen delivery of food to the *Potemkin.* *(Cut to . . .)*	841 / **B8**	LS *63*
The citizens gathered on the Odessa steps are seen in closer view. Many wave. *(Cut to . . .)*	842 / **B9**	LS *29*
The woman wearing pince-nez and the young girl smile happily. The girl waves. *(Cut to . . .)*	843 / **C2**	CU *46*
An elegant woman, wearing a dark, fashionable jacket and feathered hat, watches the offscreen battleship through her lorgnette. She raises her veil, smiles enthusiastically and waves the lorgnette. *(Cut to . . .)*	844 / **B10**	CU *69*
A handsome woman in white, wearing dark wristlets and a smart straw hat, twirls the beribboned parasol on her shoulder and waves. *(Cut to . . .)*	845 / **B11**	CU *53*

844

846

The figures of two elegantly dressed women are seen from the waist down as they stand near each other on the steps. One woman opens the light-colored parasol she carries and raises it out of the frame. Abruptly, in the space between them appears a young cripple whose legs are severed at the hips. He propels himself like a giant crab on blocks of wood held in his hands. He, too, waves toward the battleship offscreen. *(Cut to . . .)*

846 / MS
B12 *128*

The woman with the feathered hat and lorgnette continues to smile and wave her approval. *(Cut to . . .)*

847 / CU
B13 *32*

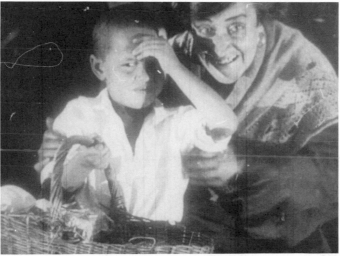

849

854

85!

The legless cripple squatting on the steps between the two smartly dressed figures pulls off his cap and waves it. *(Cut to . . .)*   848 / MS   **B14** *52*

On the steps, a boy holding a basket peers toward the camera. His young mother, wearing gold hoop earrings and a shawl over her shoulders, bends into the frame toward him to point to the offscreen battleship. *(Cut to . . .)*   849 / CU   **E1** *47*

(From below) The white flag of the *Potemkin*'s crew whips briskly from the highest flagstaff on the battleship. It is a revolutionary banner uniting all who see it from the battleship, the yawls, and the shore. *(Cut to . . .)*   850 / LS   **D19** *39*

The mother of the young boy tells him what the sailors have achieved against their officers. She gently removes the basket from his arm and urges him to wave his greetings to the *Potemkin* as she is doing. *(Cut to . . .)*   851 / CU   **E2** *110*

Two children, raised on high by adult hands cut off by the bottom frame, wave and smile cheerfully. Behind them, hats fly up into the air. *(Cut to . . .)*   852 / CU   **B15** *74*

The upper frame line cuts through the figures of four citizens, two women and two men, standing on different steps. One woman holds a white parasol. *(Cut to . . .)*   853 / MS   **B16** *30*

Suddenly . . . *(Cut to . . .)*   TITLE *78*

The dark hairdo of a woman fills the screen from frame edge to frame edge. Blurred with swift movement, it jerks away   854 / ECU   **B17** *7*

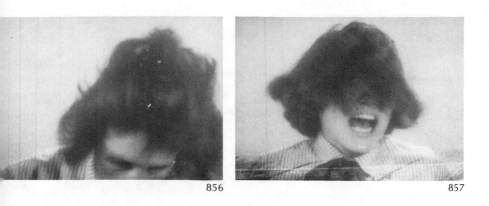

856 857

from the camera. *(Cut to . . .)*

The woman is reacting violently to an intolerable revelation. Her bobbed hair lashes about her face, hiding her eyes and brow. Only her mouth is exposed, open wide to scream. *(Cut to . . .)*	855 / **B18**	ECU 5
The woman's wildly threshing hair swirls about with blurred motion as her head again flashes toward the camera. *(Cut to . . .)*	856 / **B19**	ECU 8
The woman's flying hair and distorted face fill the frame. All control is gone. She is in utter panic. *(Cut to . . .)*	857 / **B20**	ECU 10
The legless cripple scuttles down the steps past the two elegant women. His body, supported by his powerful arms, swings like a pendulum as he flees. People hurry after him. The woman with the parasol runs toward the camera until its white circle fills the screen. *(Cut to . . .)*	858 / **B21**	MS 79
Running citizens sweep down the steps. The legless cripple makes giant leaps down the larger stone blocks which border the stairs, landing on his outthrust hands. He swivels around to look upward for a moment, then vaults down after the people. *(Cut to . . .)*	859 / **B22**	MS 84
(From above) At the top of the steps, a bronze statue with outstretched arm overlooks the long descent. For a moment only the backs of the escaping citizens can be seen. Then in the foreground a line of white-jacketed, black-booted troops carrying rifles with fixed bayonets appears at the top of the	860 / **F1**	LS 58

steps. *(Cut to . . .)*

A swirl of civilian feet bolt down the stairs. Among them, a woman who has tripped and fallen gets up and continues her flight. *(Cut to . . .)*	861 / **B23**	MS *38*
(Looking toward the steps) The immense sweep ⌐f the rising Odessa steps fills the screen. The upper levels are crowded with civilians rushing down the stairs to escape from the troops above. As the civilians reach the lower levels they fan out. *(Cut to . . .)*	862 / **B24**	LS *100*
Cut by the upper frame line, two feet standing on a step slowly sag into the frame, followed by buckling knees. *(Cut to . . .)*	863 / **B25**	CU *45*
The body of another civilian falls through the air, the arc of movement blurred by the camera's simultaneous downward thrust. *(Cut to . . .)*	864 / **B26**	MS *11*
The flying body of the second casualty lands in a sprawl	865 /	CU

across a step. *(Cut to . . .)* **B27** *15*

Matching the position of the sprawling body seen in the previous shot, the buckling knees of the first wounded civilian sag sideways out of the frame. *(Cut to . . .)* 866 / CU **B28** 6

The first wounded civilian falls across a step. Behind him, another citizen collapses in a heap. A young boy, his descent blocked by the first body, sits down in confusion and places his hands to his ears to shut out the sounds of firing. He screams. *(Cut to . . .)* 867 / MS **B29** *38*

Two flights of empty steps are suddenly covered with civilians racing downward to escape the guns of the soldiers above them. *(Cut to . . .)* 868 / MS **B30** *115*

The crowd pours down the Odessa steps, dashing past a prostrate body. Another civilian falls near it. *(Cut to . . .)* 869 / MS **B31** *44*

(Down the steps) Near the bronze statue, the first line of 870 / LS

armed troops starts down the stairs. Behind them, another line of soldiers appears, their guns pointing at the civilians. *(Cut to . . .)*   **F2**   *44*

The camera moves downward along the edge of the steps, following a horde of men running frantically to escape the gunfire. Some throw up their arms and fall headlong. *(Cut to . . .)*   871 / **B32**   LS *19*

Three women huddle horror-stricken at the side of the steps. Two of them, a refined woman wearing pince-nez and her younger companion, have been seen previously. The spectacled woman presses her hands to her ears. *(Cut to . . .)*   872 / **C3**   CU *30*

In an area of the steps seen from the side, dozens of fleeing civilians sweep past. A one-legged man on crutches painfully lurches by. In the far distance, ships can be seen at anchor in the harbor. *(Cut to . . .)*   873 / **B33**   MS *67*

A man and a woman huddle behind a stone parapet on the stairs. They gaze anxiously offscreen. *(Cut to . . .)*   874 / **B34**   CU *26*

Two crouching men and a woman peer out from behind a protecting block of stone. Suddenly, one of the men staggers   875 / **B35**   CU *40*

873

882

backward and falls in fright against the other. *(Cut to . . .)*

(Down the steps) Below the bronze statue, the troops halt and raise their rifles to fire at the fleeing crowd. *(Cut to . . .)* 876 / LS **F3** 39

The man and woman watching apprehensively from behind a stone parapet react violently to the shots. He falls backward against her. She grasps his knee as her hat flies off. *(Cut to . . .)* 877 / CU **B36** 36

In another area of the steps seen from the side, men, women, and children pour past the camera in a mad rush. *(Cut to . . .)* 878 / MS **B37** 49

A pair of white-trousered legs steps quickly over the head and shoulders of an older man prostrate on a step. He raises his head and stares about him in a daze. *(Cut to . . .)* 879 / CU **B38** 36

Running figures stream past the camera as they race down the steps. Many fall and roll. *(Cut to . . .)* 880 / LS **B39** 45

The dazed older man, panic-stricken, buries his head in his hands. *(Cut to . . .)* 881 / CU **B40** 27

As the camera moves downward along the side of the steps it keeps pace with escaping civilians. Among them, nearest 882 / MS **E3** 74

883

the camera, is the shawled young mother who had urged her son to wave toward the *Potemkin*. *(Cut to . . .)*

The rifles of the troops at the top of the steps point downward across the frame. Smoke bursts from the guns as they are fired into the crowd of civilians. *(Cut to . . .)*	883 / **F4**	CU *23*
The feet of the mother hurry down the steps past the camera. The boy at her side falls headlong, unnoticed. *(Cut to . . .)*	884 / **E4**	MS *21*
The camera moves down the steps, following the young mother who is unaware that her child has been hurt. *(Cut to . . .)*	885 / **E5**	LS *30*
The boy's face and shoulders fill the screen. Blood streams down his brow and has spattered over his shirt. His eyes are squeezed tightly shut as he cries out for help. *(Cut to . . .)*	886 / **E6**	CU *20*
The moving camera continues to follow the running mother down the steps. It halts as she stops, suddenly aware that her son is no longer at her side. She turns quickly and looks back up the steps. *(Cut to . . .)*	887 / **E7**	LS *46*
Her eyes search anxiously for her son. She screams as she sees him. *(Cut to . . .)*	888 / **E8**	CU *26*

The boy wails again for his mother. Suddenly his body goes limp and his bloody head drops to the step. *(Cut to . . .)* 889 / CU **E9** *42*

The boy's mother presses her hands against her temples in horror. *(Cut to . . .)* 890 / CU **E10** *9*

The boy's body, prostrate on the steps, is almost kicked by the frightened civilians leaping awkwardly over him. *(Cut to . . .)* 891 / MS **E11** *42*

The mother's panic-stricken face fills the screen, her eyes distended, her mouth open in dazed, intense pain. She moves closer to the camera. *(Cut to . . .)* 892 / ECU **E12** *14*

Young boys and men gallop down the steps, escaping unharmed. *(Cut to . . .)* 893 / MS **B41** *42*

The fallen boy's legs rest on a deeply eroded step. A pair of legs in white trousers, cut by the frame, steps roughly over the child's body. *(Cut to . . .)* 894 / CU **E13** *25*

A heavy black shoe callously grinds into the child's extended hand as it moves past. *(Cut to . . .)*

895 / ECU
E14 *28*

The boy's mother, clutching her hair in frenzy, advances straight at the camera until her brow fills the screen. *(Cut to . . .)*

896 / CU
E15 *27*

891

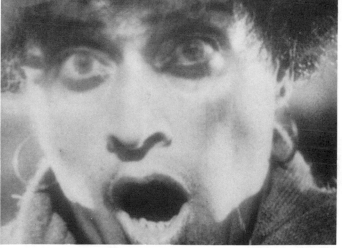

892

897

The escaping horde races down the steps. A young man among them suddenly clutches his chest, stops, and begins to lose his balance. *(Cut to . . .)* — 897 / B42 — MS 32

Another group scatters down the steps, men leading women, older people fleeing feebly. *(Cut to . . .)* — 898 / B43 — MS 39

A man's heavy shoe roughly brushes the boy's bloody shoulder in passing, jostling the body and rolling it to another step. *(Cut to . . .)* — 899 / E16 — ECU 41

The boy's body rolls over on its back, the head resting on a lower step than the feet. A pair of women's neatly cleaned white shoes walks across his chest. *(Cut to . . .)* — 900 / E17 — ECU 26

The mother's frenzied face pushes toward the camera until her horror-struck eyes almost fill the screen. *(Cut to . . .)* — 901 / E18 — ECU 24

The panicky citizens continue their flight down the steps. The young man who had earlier begun to lose his balance falls to the pavement and is engulfed by the crowd. *(Cut to . . .)* — 902 / B44 — MS 26

The boy's mother is surrounded by sympathetic people who move up the stairs with her toward her child. Suddenly their desire to help is swept away by fear. They turn and run — 903 / E19 — MS 88 down the steps leaving her alone, staring down at her son's body. *(Cut to . . .)*

The boy is sprawled across the steps. His crushed hand casts a stark shadow on the stone. *(Cut to . . .)*	904 / CU **E20**	18

The mother bends down out of the frame. Beyond her, the feet of women fly downward over the broad stone steps. *(Cut to . . .)*	905 / MS **E21**	18

Civilians flee down the stairs. Some scatter to the sides, but most dash toward the bottom of the vast series of steps. *(Cut to . . .)*	906 / LS **B45**	62

The mother rises into the frame carrying her boy in her arms. She starts to move upward against the tide of frightened people surging past, then stops for a moment, turns and shrieks to the people around her. *(Cut to . . .)*	907 / MS **E22**	69

The populace continues to pour in panic over the enormous steps. Bodies are now lying all about, shot down by the implacable rifles of the approaching troops. *(Cut to . . .)*	908 / LS **B46**	79

The woman wearing pince-nez and her companion huddle	909 / MS

907

against the shelter of a stone parapet adjoining the steps. The woman starts to rise to her knees. *(Cut to . . .)*	**C4**	*33*

The woman rises and presses both palms together with a resolute gesture. *(Cut to . . .)* — 910 / CU **C5** *28*

Standing, the woman vigorously clutches both ends of her white shawl and speaks to her companion. *(Cut to . . .)* — 911 / ECU **C6** *27*

An area of the steps near the stone parapet is seen from the side. The steps are littered with dead bodies lying in grotesquely distorted positions. Across the frame moves the distraught mother carrying her child up the stairs. She is bereft, agonized, wailing. She hesitates on a step, turns and cries out in her grief to those below her. *(Cut to . . .)* — 912 / MS **E23** *70*

The woman with pince-nez reaches out her hands in supplication to those around her. *(Cut to . . .)* — 913 / CU **C7** *43*

"Let us appeal to them!" *(Cut to . . .)* — TITLE *109*

The woman looks about to see who will join her in the appeal. *(Cut to . . .)* — 914 / CU **C8** *15*

A crowd of civilians surges down the steps, blind and deaf — 915 / MS

911

912

to everything except escape to safety. *(Cut to . . .)* **B47** *45*

The woman wearing pince-nez rises to her feet as her terror- 916 / CU
stricken neighbors crawl toward her and gather about her **C9** *55*
like frightened children. *(Cut to . . .)*

The fear-stricken faces of five men and women look up 917 / CU
anxiously at the offscreen woman who has dared to take **C10** *40*

920

action. *(Cut to . . .)*

The woman looks down at her offscreen companions and smiles reassuringly. Then she turns to look up the stairs to assess the task ahead. *(Cut to . . .)*	918 / CU **C11** 38
The five faces turn apprehensively to the left, following the confident gaze of their leader. *(Cut to . . .)*	919 / CU **C12** 25
A line of long, menacing shadows cast by the approaching offscreen troops crawls slowly downward across the empty steps. Finally, the black-booted troops appear at the upper steps. They descend in slow, steady cadence, rifles gripped in firing position. *(Cut to . . .)*	920 / LS **F5** 66
(From above) The mother carrying her child advances up the steps toward the camera, wildly berating the troops for their murderous cruelty. *(Cut to . . .)*	921 / CU **E24** 30
The apprehensive faces of two of the crouching women about to appeal to the troops fill the screen. One turns away hesitantly out of the frame. The other begins to rise slowly, drawn by a will stronger than her fear. *(Cut to . . .)*	922 / ECU **C13** 63

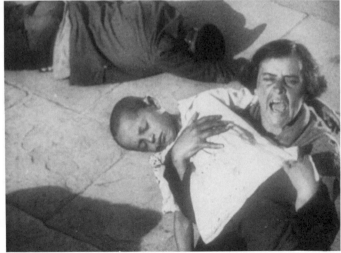

921

The face of the woman wearing pince-nez beams with courage and confidence as she urges her neighbors to follow her example. *(Cut to . . .)*

923 / CU
C14 26

The crouching younger woman clutches her shirt fearfully but prepares to join the appeal to the troops. She begins to rise. *(Cut to . . .)*

924 / ECU
C15 35

The young woman stands and moves out of the frame. Two men bent in panic beside her also begin to rise. *(Cut to . . .)*

925 / ECU
C16 36

The two men in the group raise themselves from a crouching position, their backs to the camera. *(Cut to . . .)*

926 / CU
C17 14

Another woman huddled near the two men also begins to rise to join the appeal. *(Cut to . . .)*

927 / CU
C18 18

The six protesters move timidly to the left out of the frame, followed by a one-legged man on crutches. *(Cut to . . .)*

928 / MS
C19 50

The line of advancing troops halts at a broad step and fires at the offscreen civilians. Bursts of rifle smoke drift back over the soldiers. *(Cut to . . .)*

929 / MS
F6 26

934

(Down the steps) Men run frantically down the steps away from the slowly moving camera to escape the brutal volley of bullets. *(Cut to . . .)* 930 / LS **B48** 42

The camera moves with the mother as she carries her child up the steps. Purged of fear by her loss, she shrieks at the troops in hatred. *(Cut to . . .)* 931 / CU **E25** 39

The camera moves up the steps with the small group of supplicants led by the woman wearing pince-nez. Some hold their arms wide in pleading. *(Cut to . . .)* 932 / CU **C20** 56

The mother carrying her child continues to climb up the steps toward the troops, crying out her agonized protest. The camera moves with her. *(Cut to . . .)* 933 / ECU **E26** 40

The enormous shadows of the advancing soldiers stretch ominously across a broad landing between two flights of steps. The soldiers move into the frame from the left, rifles at hips, striding with measured gait over the dead bodies lying about. They continue down the next flight of the vast stairway. *(Cut to . . .)* 934 / MS **F7** 80

The broad flight of steps is strewn with slaughtered men, women, and children. As the black boots of the descending soldiers appear at the top, the mother with her son's body comes into view from the bottom. *(Cut to . . .)* 935 / MS **E27** 77

"Listen to me! Don't shoot!" *(Cut to . . .)* TITLE 101

The camera looks down the steps, which cut the screen diagonally. The line of soldiers, cut off at chest level by the top frame, moves into full view and continues to descend with measured cadence. *(Cut to . . .)* 936 / MS **F8** 76

The mother bearing her child ascends the steps through the litter of dead bodies, moving toward the offscreen troops. Midway, the camera begins to move with her. As she advances, the long shadows cast by the soldiers standing motionless above her come into view. Keeping the mother in the center of the frame, the camera pans across the elongated shadows and comes to the soldiers and an officer with 937 / LS **E28** 217

935

937

arm raised to give the order to fire. *(Cut to . . .)*

"My child is hurt!" *(Cut to . . .)*   TITLE   *84*

The camera continues to move past the line of soldiers in the   938 / LS
immediate foreground who, with rifles to their shoulders,   **E29**   *67*
await their officer's signal to fire. The mother stops close to
them and stands facing the troops with her child in her arms.
(Cut to . . .)

The group of pleaders led by the woman wearing pince-nez   939 / CU
advances with arms outstretched as the camera follows   **C21**   *60*
alongside. *(Cut to . . .)*

The officer signals. The soldiers fire. Smoke erupts from the   940 / LS
rifle muzzles, momentarily obscuring the figure of the   **E30**   *22*
mother. *(Cut to . . .)*

The body of the mother, partially cut off by the top frame,   941 / CU
crumples slowly across the soldiers' shadows toward the   **E31**   *15*
ground. *(Cut to . . .)*

Fleeing civilians run past a wall adjoining the bottom of the   942 / MS
Odessa steps. Two cavalrymen gallop by close to the cam-   **G1**   *52*

942

era, briefly blocking the scene behind them. *(Cut to . . .)*

The mother's body sags backward and she falls across the soldiers' shadows. Her son lies sprawled on top of her. Her hands relax their grip and drop limply to her side. *(Cut to . . .)* | 943 / **E32** | CU 72 |

Cossacks *(Cut to . . .)* — TITLE 57

Galloping horses race past, so close to the camera that their flanks fill the screen. Beyond them, civilians scatter at the bottom of the steps. *(Cut to . . .)* — 944 / **G2** MS 56

The bottom flights of the Odessa steps swarm with fleeing civilians who veer suddenly to avoid the new threat that hems off their escape. Cossacks on horseback race into view and slash at the people around them. *(Cut to . . .)* — 945 / **G3** LS 93

The long line of troops descends implacably across the steps, stepping over the prostrate bodies of the mother and her son as they advance. *(Cut to . . .)* — 946 / **E33** LS 119

At a railing near the bottom of the Odessa steps, a man's figure collapses to the ground while an elderly man struggles — 947 / **G4** MS 76

945

950

to lift an old woman. Another man cartwheels violently over the railing, falls, rolls, and lies still. In the far background, Cossack horsemen and civilians mill about frantically. *(Cut to . . .)*

(From above) Led by the woman with pince-nez, the small group of pleaders hesitates near a lamppost at the side of the steps. *(Cut to . . .)*	948 / **C22**	MS 16
(From below) A dozen firing rifles slash the screen diagonally from upper left to lower right. *(Cut to . . .)*	949 / **F9**	CU 14
(From above) All in the group of pleaders except the woman wearing pince-nez fling themselves to the pavement. *(Cut to . . .)*	950 / **C23**	MS 39
(From below) Having fired, the soldiers again resume their implacable march down the steps. Partially cut by the frame, they move past the camera. *(Cut to . . .)*	951 / **F10**	CU 27
A young mother in a black lace shawl, hurriedly pushing her baby in its white carriage, approaches the top step of one of the flights. She hesitates over the risky descent and halts to fasten her child securely. Civilians flee past down the steps. A young woman among them accidentally collides with the carriage from the rear. The agitated mother pushes	952 / **H1**	MS 92

952

her away and turns fearfully to look back at the troops. *(Cut to . . .)*

The soldiers march slowly, irresistibly, across the screen from left to right as their measured cadence carries them down the steps. *(Cut to . . .)*	953 / **F11**	MS 44
The young mother, her face edged by the black lace shawl, stares apprehensively offscreen. She bites her lip in indecision. *(Cut to . . .)*	954 / **H2**	ECU 39
Her white-gloved hand trembles and picks agitatedly at the edge of the luxurious carriage. *(Cut to . . .)*	955 / **H3**	ECU 42
The young mother stands tensely between her baby and the approaching offscreen soldiers. *(Cut to . . .)*	956 / **H4**	MS 35
She cries out piteously as she realizes that her baby is trapped between the advancing soldiers and the steep steps before her. *(Cut to . . .)*	957 / **H5**	ECU 20
Five empty steps stretch across the screen. A line of black boots advances across the top step in unison and marches slowly, steadily downward. *(Cut to . . .)*	958 / **F12**	CU 50
(From below) Smoke erupts from a line of rifles silhouetted against the sky as they are fired. *(Cut to . . .)*	959 / **F13**	CU 20

The young mother's head sways back. Her eyes close as her mouth opens in mortal agony. *(Cut to . . .)*

958
960 / ECU
H6 *42*

The front wheels of the baby carriage roll slightly forward and teeter for a moment at the edge of the step. *(Cut to . . .)*

961 / ECU
H7 *30*

The mother's eyes are glazed with shock. Her head sways

962 / ECU

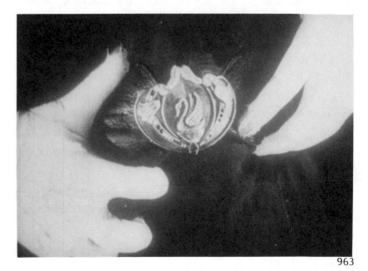

963

forward; her mouth hangs open. *(Cut to . . .)*　　**H8**　　*52*

The mother's gloved hands slowly move toward the large　963 / ECU
silver-buckled belt at her waist. They clutch spasmodically　**H9**　　*82*
at the buckle. *(Cut to . . .)*

The mounted Cossacks at the bottom of the steps slash at　964 /　LS
the civilians nearest them. The fleeing citizens are in utter　**G5**　　*66*
panic, running in all directions. The steps are littered with
dead and wounded. *(Cut to . . .)*

Blood drips over the mother's belt and silver buckle. Her　965 / ECU
bloody, gloved hands twitch in pain at her waist. *(Cut*　**H10**　　*46*
to . . .)

The mother's body begins to sag to the steps. Her hands　966 /　CU
clutch feebly at her wound. *(Cut to . . .)*　　**H11**　　*20*

Eyes glazed, mouth loosely open, the mother's face sways　967 / ECU
across the screen. Her eyes close and her head sinks slowly　**H12**　　*87*
out of the frame. *(Cut to . . .)*

The mother's sagging shoulders and belted waist fill the　968 /　CU
screen. Behind her, as she sinks out of the frame, the　**H13**　　*93*

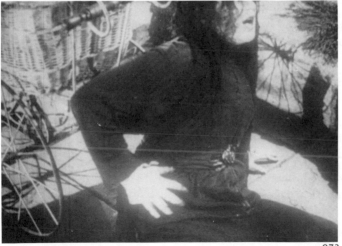

973

baby in the carriage stretches out its hands. People rush by on the steps. *(Cut to . . .)*

The front wheels of the baby carriage roll nearer to the edge of the worn stone landing on which they rest. *(Cut to . . .)*	969 / **H14**	ECU 28
In a deadly cadence, the black boots of a long line of soldiers descend five steps that stretch diagonally across the screen and move out of the frame. *(Cut to . . .)*	970 / **F14**	CU 30
(From below) In the same cadence as the previous shot, the white jackets of the soldiers move across the screen and out of the frame. *(Cut to . . .)*	971 / **F15**	CU 32
(From above) The mother clutches weakly at her waist and sags toward the landing. *(Cut to . . .)*	972 / **H15**	CU 24
(From above) Now nearer to the landing, the mother falls back against the baby carriage behind her. *(Cut to . . .)*	973 / **H16**	CU 38
The rear wheels of the baby carriage roll out of the frame to the left as it heads down the steps. *(Cut to . . .)*	974 / **H17**	ECU 9
The front wheels of the carriage stand motionless at the center of a step. *(Cut to . . .)*	975 / **H18**	ECU 6
The Odessa steps rise across the screen. They swarm with civilians escaping the two lines of troops near the top. *(Cut to . . .)*	976 / **F16**	LS 11
At the bottom of the steps the wild melee continues between civilians and mounted Cossacks. *(Cut to . . .)*	977 / **G6**	LS 32
Near the railing off to one side of the bottom steps, the white-haired man continues to tug helplessly at his wife lying on the ground. *(Cut to . . .)*	978 / **G7**	MS 23
The lace-shawled mother falls backward to the landing, pushing her baby's carriage down the steps out of the frame. *(Cut to . . .)*	979 / **H19**	CU 11
(From overhead) The carriage rolls diagonally across the screen from bottom right to upper left. *(Cut to . . .)*	980 / **H20**	ECU 17

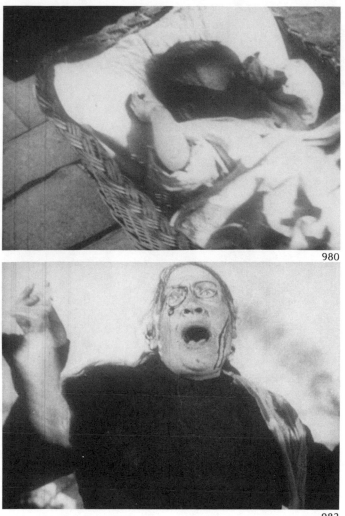

980

982

The large rear wheels of the carriage roll over the edge of the landing and out of the frame as the body of the baby's mother sinks prostrate behind it to the ground. *(Cut to . . .)*

981 / ECU
H21 *14*

The woman wearing pince-nez stands with hands upraised in horror. Rivulets of blood run across her jaw. Her hat and white shawl have fallen off her head. *(Cut to . . .)*

982 / CU
C24 *7*

(From above) The baby carriage jounces its way slowly
down the steps past many bodies. The camera moves with
it. *(Cut to . . .)*

983 / CU
H22   46

The carriage enters the screen from the left, slowly, awkwardly rolling down a flight of steps littered with dead and

984 / MS
H23   38

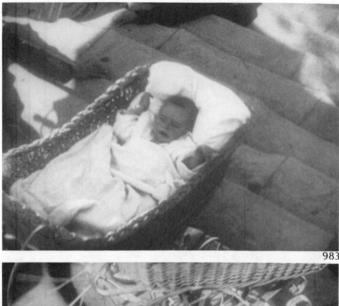

983

991

wounded. Fleeing civilians hurry past it as they escape down the steps.

Across a landscape of steps almost obscured by the dead, the runaway baby carriage enters the screen at the upper left. It bounces downward from step to step, ignored by the imperiled citizens around it. *(Cut to . . .)*	985 / **H24**	LS 72
A larger number of Cossacks on horseback now pursue the civilians across the broad area at the base of the steps. *(Cut to . . .)*	986 / **G8**	LS 41
The mother of the baby in the carriage lies dead on the ground. Her head extends over the edge of the landing. *(Cut to . . .)*	987 / **H25**	CU 15
(From above) The carriage continues its uneven, bouncing progress down the steps, the camera moving with it past dead bodies. *(Cut to . . .)*	988 / **H26**	CU 25
The horror-struck face of the woman wearing pince-nez fills the screen. Her jaw is bloody, her hair disheveled. Her mouth open, she stares offscreen. *(Cut to . . .)*	989 / **C25**	ECU 21
From a slightly different position, the distraught woman continues to stare offscreen. Her eyes widen slightly. *(Cut to . . .)*	990 / **C26**	ECU 10
(From the side) With the camera moving alongside, the carriage wheels bump down the stone steps at a swifter pace. They roll over an extended arm and an abandoned hat. *(Cut to . . .)*	991 / **H27**	CU 49
A young man, his head pressed close to the frame of a mirror, gasps in shock at what he sees offscreen. *(Cut to . . .)*	992 / **H28**	CU 13
The elderly white-haired man striving to lift his companion from the ground is bumped by the falling body of a young man who has just hurdled over the railing nearby. Cossacks and civilians mill about in the background. *(Cut to . . .)*	993 / **G9**	MS 56
(From above) The speeding baby carriage rolls swiftly across a landing, the camera moving with it. *(Cut to . . .)*	994 / **H29**	CU 28

995

The young man follows the course of the offscreen carriage with shocked eyes, his moving head doubled by the mirror against which he leans. *(Cut to . . .)* — 995 / CU **H30** *25*

The moving camera follows the jouncing carriage as it rolls rapidly down the steps and across a landing. *(Cut to . . .)* — 996 / CU **H31** *28*

(From above) The baby's body rocks violently in the carriage as it slowly rolls out of the frame. *(Cut to . . .)* — 997 / ECU **H32** *27*

With the camera moving alongside, the carriage wheels bounce down the stone steps at a swift pace, rolling over an extended limb. *(Cut to . . .)* — 998 / CU **H33** *23*

(From above) The baby's body jostles to and fro in the carriage. *(Cut to . . .)* — 999 / ECU **H34** *10*

Three pairs of soldiers' boots, cut by the upper frame, stand nonchalantly poised on two steps, above a heap of dead and dying civilians. Two bare arms stretch piteously into the screen from below. Three rifles with fixed bayonets point downward at the bodies. A burst of smoke erupts from the guns and drifts across the screen. *(Cut to . . .)* — 1000 / CU **F17** *19*

The young man standing at the mirror screams. His head and its reflected image fill the screen. *(Cut to . . .)* — 1001 / ECU **H35** *6*

1000

The baby carriage whips across the screen in a blur of motion. *(Cut to . . .)*

1002 / CU
H36   9

(From the side) With the camera moving alongside, the carriage wheels bounce down the stone steps, rolling over an extended arm. *(Cut to . . .)*

1003 / CU
H37   17

1006

1007

100

1009

101

(From directly above) The baby in the carriage is carried swiftly across a landing. The camera moves with it at a slower pace. *(Cut to . . .)*	1004 / **H38**	MS	27
The young man at the mirror cranes his neck to follow the action. *(Cut to . . .)*	1005 / **H39**	ECU	13
(From behind) The baby carriage rolling down the steps suddenly tilts forward and begins to flip, rear over front. *(Cut to . . .)*	1006 / **H40**	CU	13
(From below) A young officer starts to swing his sabre from high above his left shoulder. *(Cut to . . .)*	1007 / **C27**	CU	6
The officer's violent grimace and upper arm fill the screen as his offscreen sabre slashes downward. *(Cut to . . .)*	1008 / **C28**	ECU	8
The officer's snarling face fills the screen. *(Cut to . . .)*	1009 / **C29**	ECU	1

The officer's arm swings swiftly back across his shoulder and starts down again as he shouts in murderous fury. *(Cut to . . .)*

1010 / ECU
C30   16

The face of the woman wearing pince-nez fills the screen. Her glasses now hang awry on her nose, the right lens shattered. Blood spurts from her right eye and runs down her face. Her mouth gapes in shock and horror. *(Fade out and cut to . . .)*

1011 / ECU
C31   48

A giant cannon on the *Potemkin* slowly swings toward the camera. *(Cut to . . .)*

1012 / MS
D20   67

The brutal military power answered by the guns of the battleship. *(Cut to . . .)*

TITLE   174

(Head on) The muzzles of two giant cannon stare straight at the camera like menacing eyes. Behind the turret looms the empty bridge and bold superstructure of the *Potemkin.* *(Cut to . . .)*

1013 / LS
D21   36

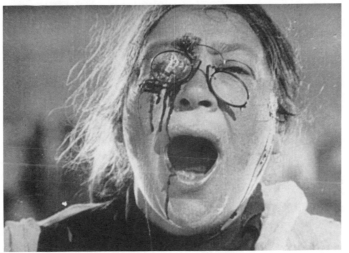

1011

1012

1013

Target! The Odessa Theatre *(Cut to . . .)* TITLE   *101*

A large sculpture group, goddess and chariot surrounded by leopards, stands silhouetted against the sky. *(Cut to . . .)* 1014 / MS
I 1   *27*

The headquarters of the generals! *(Cut to . . .)* TITLE   *105*

From one of the *Potemkin*'s side turret guns a huge white 1015 / LS

1014

1015

mushroom of smoke bursts forth and blows away. *(Cut to . . .)* **D22** *40*

(From below) A decorative stone cherub perches on a cornice silhouetted against the sky. *(Cut to . . .)* 1016 / MS **I 2** *7*

(From below) Another stone cherub embellishing a cornice is silhouetted against the sky. *(Cut to . . .)* 1017 / MS **I 3** *7*

1022

(From below) A third cherub sculpture nestles benignly at a corner of a building. *(Cut to . . .)* — 1018 / MS I 4   4

A tall, ornamental iron gate supported by heavy stone piers is hit by a shell and begins to topple. *(Cut to . . .)* — 1019 / LS I 5   21

The toppling gate is seen from a different camera position. Billowing smoke obscures the falling fragments. *(Cut to . . .)* — 1020 / LS I 6   9

The crumbling gate and stone piers, seen from a different viewpoint, are buried in the smoke of another bursting shell. *(Cut to . . .)* — 1021 / LS I 7   30

A sculptured stone lion sleeping on its forepaws fills the screen. *(Cut to . . .)* — 1022 / CU I 8   10

A stone lion with head alertly raised fills the screen. *(Cut to . . .)* — 1023 / CU I 9   14

(From below) A stone lion, aroused and standing on its forelegs, towers against the smoke-filled sky. *(Cut to . . .)* — 1024 / CU I 10   17

The upper portion of the entrance gate and supporting stone pier of the headquarters stands silhouetted against the sky. *(Cut to . . .)* — 1025 / MS I 11   7

1023

1024

Billowing, churning clouds of dark grey smoke fill the
screen. *(Cut to . . .)*

Clouds of dark smoke cut through by flying debris envelop
a telegraph pole and building façade. *(Cut to . . .)*

The top of a tower, barely visible behind the violently billowing dark smoke and falling debris, disappears in the

1026 / CU
I 12   *9*

1027 / LS
I 13   *17*

1028 / LS
I 14   *24*

erupting clouds as it starts to fall. *(Cut to . . .)*

The churning grey smoke clears momentarily to reveal part of the iron gate leading to the generals' headquarters. *(Cut and fade in to . . .)*

1029 / LS
I 15   37

PART V
MEETING THE SQUADRON *(Fade out and cut to . . .)*

TITLE   93

Till evening a stormy meeting went on. *(Cut to . . .)*

TITLE   96

In the foreground, two sailors with their backs to the camera address their shipmates crowded on the *Potemkin*'s quarterdeck below them. One of the speakers turns and looks upward. *(Cut to . . .)*

1030 / MS
A1   68

(From below) The crow's nest, high on the *Potemkin*'s mast, is jammed with attentive sailors. *(Cut to . . .)*

1031 / LS
A2   48

The speaker directs his remarks to the men on the mast with enormous, earthy vigor, swinging his arms to emphasize his views. *(Cut to . . .)*

1032 / CU
A3   69

"The people of Odessa await their deliverers. The citizens and soldiers will join you." *(Cut to . . .)*

TITLE   229

The sailor finishes his speech to the seamen above and turns back to face the group on the deck below. *(Cut to . . .)*

1033 / CU
A4   70

(From below) The turret, bridge, and mast, rising in graduated levels, are thronged with sailors meeting to decide their next move. There is a stir at the stairs leading to the bridge. *(Cut to . . .)*

1034 / LS
A5   84

(From below) A group of sailors push one of their shipmates up the stairway leading to the bridge. He climbs up beside the first speaker. *(Cut to . . .)*

1035 / LS
A6   67

(From above) The newcomer pushes aside the sailor who has just addressed the gathering and begins to speak with great animation, looking up toward the men on the crow's

1036 / MS
A7   78

1030

nest. *(Cut to . . .)*

He pleads his case excitedly, shouting his words to those above him. *(Cut to . . .)*	1037 / CU **A8**	53
"Landing is impossible. The squadron is on its way." *(Cut to . . .)*	TITLE	42
The sailor waves his arm vigorously to emphasize his warning. *(Cut to . . .)*	1038 / CU **A9**	35
(From above) The prow and the quarterdeck of the *Potemkin* are crowded with listening sailors. *(Cut to . . .)*	1039 / LS **A10**	51
The speaker turns his back to the camera to repeat his warning to the sailors on the different levels below him. *(Cut to . . .)*	1040 / CU **A11**	32
(From below) The sailors on the turret and the bridge respond to the news with courageous cheers. *(Cut to . . .)*	1041 / LS **A12**	43
(From above) The deck of the *Potemkin* bristles with waving caps as the crewmen unanimously support the speaker. *(Cut to . . .)*	1042 / LS **A13**	39
The new speaker, his back to the camera, continues to press for action against the Czarist fleet. *(Cut to . . .)*	1043 / CU **A14**	30

The previous speaker stands silently to one side, arms crossed, chin on fist, listening. He turns to observe the crew's willingness to fight. *(Cut to . . .)*	1044 / **A15**	CU *54*
The new speaker faces the camera and shouts to the sailors above him. *(Cut to . . .)*	1045 / **A16**	CU *21*
(From above) The second speaker claps the first one on the shoulder, turns him around and vigorously pleads with him to change his mind. After a moment the first sailor agrees, making a friendly gesture of assent. *(Cut to . . .)*	1046 / **A17**	MS *138*
With one voice they decided to meet the squadron. *(Cut to . . .)*	TITLE	*133*
(From below) The sailors in the crow's nest wave their caps in grim approval of the decision. *(Cut to . . .)*	1047 / **A18**	LS *33*
(From above) The waving, cheering crew on the prow and	1048 /	LS

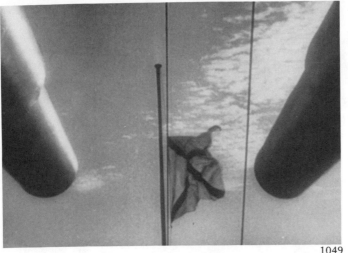

1049

the quarterdeck of the *Potemkin* disappears in a film dissolve. The decks are now bare, stripped for action, ready for the danger ahead. *(Fade out and cut to . . .)*	A19	74
The night came, full of anxieties. *(Cut to . . .)*	TITLE	92
Two main guns of the *Potemkin* point toward the evening sky. The battleship's flag is lowered slowly from the top of the staff. *(Cut to . . .)*	1049 / LS B1	145
Trees on the far horizon stand silhouetted against dark, towering clouds that hide the moon. *(Cut to . . .)*	1050 / LS B2	103
The moon throws a long path of glittering light across the water. In the far distance, a yawl quietly glides like a black bird across the silvery surface. *(Cut to . . .)*	1051 / LS B3	125
On the bridge of the *Potemkin,* an armed sentry is silhouetted against the dancing glints of moonlight as he scans the horizon. *(Cut to . . .)*	1052 / MS B4	68
Underneath a dark vault of sky, moonlit breakers tumble quietly over an endless beach. *(Cut to . . .)*	1053 / LS B5	95
The sentry on the bridge turns and paces forward on his vigil. *(Cut to . . .)*	1054 / MS B6	52
The gleaming waves sweep over the beach under the omi-	1055 / LS	

nous, dark sky. *(Cut to . . .)*	**B7**	*58*

(From below) Two armed sentries slowly pace their watch on different deck levels of the *Potemkin.* (Cut to . . .) — 1056 / LS **B8** *70*

The battleship rides at anchor like a huge horned beast alert to the approach of danger. Its three funnels are silhouetted against the evening sky. *(Cut to . . .)* — 1057 / LS **B9** *32*

In the engineroom two large dial indicators stand at zero. *(Cut to . . .)* — 1058 / CU **C1** *26*

Seven other control dials in the engineroom of the sleeping ship are also at rest. *(Cut to . . .)* — 1059 / CU **C2** *21*

Two engineroom crewmen sleep quietly on a bunk deep within the ship. *(Cut to . . .)* — 1060 / CU **C3** *35*

A sailor sits alertly on deck in the darkness, his features illuminated by a strong light. He turns his head warily and looks up. *(Cut to . . .)* — 1061 / CU **B10** *64*

A huge searchlight shines directly into the camera, then slowly pivots as the sailor pushing it comes into view. *(Cut to . . .)* — 1062 / CU **B11** *88*

1058

The sailor sitting in the glare of the lamp is joined by a shipmate who grips his shoulder with comradely warmth. They both stare out into the darkness. *(Cut to . . .)*

1063 / CU
B12 *87*

The searchlight operator opens its shutters and directs the powerful beam out to sea. Its glow lights the face of his assistant on the other side of the huge prism. *(Cut to . . .)*

1064 / CU
B13 *79*

Two sailors lie huddled in sleep in their quarters. *(Cut to . . .)*

1065 / CU
C4 *47*

Four engineroom control dials point to zero. The crew and the great engines of the ship rest before the trial that lies ahead. *(Cut to . . .)*

1066 / ECU
C5 *16*

The darting reflections of the moon separate and dissolve in a never-ending dance on the black, oily waters of the harbor. *(Cut to . . .)*

1067 / CU
B14 *45*

A long, low warship looms in the far distance as the quivering reflections of the moon stream across the water. *(Cut to . . .)*

1068 / LS
B15 *54*

The restless, abstract dance of moonbeams on the dark, impenetrable water mirrors the tension that surrounds the *Potemkin. (Cut to . . .)*

1069 / CU
B16 *50*

Matyushenko dozes fitfully in the glare of a harsh light on a divan in the officers' lounge. He awakes with a start, looks about and draws deeply on a cigarette stub in his hand. Disgusted with its stale flavor, he sleepily casts it away. *(Cut to . . .)*

1070 / CU
D1 *94*

Matyushenko's hand enters the frame, dropping the cigarette stub on a nearby table. Along its edge six fresh cigarettes are lined up to ease him through the long night hours. *(Cut to . . .)*

1071 / CU
D2 *25*

In the glare of the light, Matyushenko settles back on the divan for a moment, then wearily starts to rise. *(Cut to . . .)*

1072 / MS
D3 *26*

The moonlit sea is darkened by the shadow of a long plume

1073 / LS

of smoke stretching away from the *Potemkin*. A boom of the battleship juts across the screen in the foreground. *(Cut to . . .)*	**B17**	*70*
Two crewmen lie huddled in sleep in their quarters. *(Cut to . . .)*	1074 / CU **C6**	*48*
Behind the ship's helm, a sailor sits sleeping with his head on his arms. *(Cut to . . .)*	1075 / ECU **D4**	*59*
Two sailors, crowded together in an engineroom bunk, lie asleep. *(Cut to . . .)*	1076 / CU **C7**	*50*
The two sailors manning a huge searchlight on deck maintain its ceaseless revolutions. *(Cut to . . .)*	1077 / CU **B18**	*74*
A sailor lies sleeping with knees drawn up under a blanket on a couch deep in the ship. *(Cut to . . .)*	1078 / MS **E1**	*54*
On the dark bridge of the *Potemkin,* Matyushenko rouses the sleeping helmsman. *(Cut to . . .)*	1079 / CU **D5**	*58*
The sailor with the blanket drawn over his knees sleeps uncomfortably on the couch. *(Cut to . . .)*	1080 / CU **E2**	*52*
Matyushenko gives instructions to the helmsman on the bridge. They salute each other in comradely fashion and	1081 / CU **D6**	*84*

separate. The man at the helm draws on a cigarette and stands alertly at his watch. *(Cut to . . .)*

Two sleeping sailors are stretched out on a folding chair and a couch in the officers' lounge of the battleship. Cloths are drawn over the windows to shut out the glare. *(Cut to . . .)*

1082 / MS
E3   *38*

The sailor on the couch has a pillow under his head. His dark jacket is unbuttoned. *(Cut to . . .)*

1083 / CU
E4   *38*

The sailor on the folding chair rests his head heavily against his palm. *(Cut to . . .)*

1084 / CU
E5   *49*

Matyushenko enters the officers' lounge and gazes down at the sleeping pair on couch and chair. *(Cut to . . .)*

1085 / MS
D7   *59*

The dark-jacketed sailor on the couch stirs uneasily, wakes, and begins to raise himself to a sitting position. *(Cut to . . .)*

1086 / CU
D8   *51*

At the searchlight, one of the operators slowly closes down the iris and extinguishes its glare. *(Cut to . . .)*

1087 / CU
B19   *68*

In the lounge, Matyushenko talks for a moment with his dark-jacketed shipmate and then tells him to go back to sleep. The man on the couch turns and begins to settle back as Matyushenko leaves. *(Cut to . . .)*

1088 / MS
D9   *76*

The dark-jacketed sailor lies down facing the back of the couch and adjusts himself to a more comfortable sleeping position. *(Cut to . . .)*

1089 / CU
D10   *80*

A powerful light plays on the dark, unshuttered face of the huge searchlight on deck. Its operator closes the shutters and the light from offscreen moves away. *(Cut to . . .)*

1090 / CU
B20   *38*

In the officers' lounge, the sailors on the folding chair and the couch are again asleep. *(Cut to. . .)*

1091 / MS
E6   *39*

It is early dawn on deck. A sailor climbs down a metal gangway as a shipmate issues from a nearby bulkhead door. *(Cut to . . .)*

1092 / MS
B21   *68*

The two sleeping sailors stir on their bunk in the engineroom. One raises his head. *(Cut to . . .)*	1093 / **C8**	CU *28*
The sailor sleeping under a blanket suddenly moves his hand. *(Cut to . . .)*	1094 / **E7**	CU *9*
On the bridge, the helmsman adjusts a small nearby wheel. *(Cut to . . .)*	1095 / **D11**	CU *40*
On deck, the two sailors at the gangway gaze out over the ocean. *(Cut to . . .)*	1096 / **B22**	MS *34*
The two dozing sailors on the bunk in the engineroom drift between sleep and wakefulness. *(Cut to . . .)*	1097 / **C9**	MS *45*
On the bridge, the helmsman smokes his cigarette and gazes out. *(Cut to . . .)*	1098 / **D12**	CU *41*
(From below) The armed lookout at the rangefinder station on deck paces toward the camera as he searches the horizon. *(Cut to . . .)*	1099 / **B23**	MS *52*
An armed guard on deck, framed by two towering ventilators, stands alertly as the morning breeze stirs his collar. *(Cut to . . .)*	1100 / **B24**	LS *50*

1078

1101

(From below) One of the two lookouts standing at an upper observation post on the *Potemkin* lifts a telescope to his eye to observe something more intently. He lowers the glass and points out over the water as he talks to his shipmate. *(Cut to . . .)*	1101 / **B25**	LS 56
Two engineroom dials fill the screen. Their hands stand at zero. *(Cut to . . .)*	1102 / **C10**	ECU 37
Five engineroom dials fill the screen, their hands at zero. *(Cut to . . .)*	1103 / **C11**	CU 25
The armed sailor and the lookout with telescope stand guard at separate posts on deck. *(Cut to . . .)*	1104 / **B26**	LS 84
(From below) The lookout gazing through his telescope and an armed shipmate with him are momentarily blocked from view by a guard pacing by in the near foreground. *(Cut to . . .)*	1105 / **B27**	LS 91
A guard framed by a huge ventilator and a funnel raises fieldglasses to his eyes to scan more closely the waters about the battleship. *(Cut to . . .)*	1106 / **B28**	LS 79
A trailing plume of dark smoke from the *Potemkin*'s off-screen funnel stretches out across the sparkling waters. It casts a broad shadow on the waves beneath. In the fore-	1107 / **B29**	LS 50

ground, a boom of the ship extends across the screen. *(Cut to . . .)*

The armed guards and the lookout stand at their posts on deck. The sailor with the telescope continues to scan the horizon. *(Cut to . . .)*   1108 / LS **B30** *107*

The armed guard slowly paces toward the sailor with the telescope. *(Cut to . . .)*   1109 / LS **B31** *37*

(From below) The crewman lowers his glass and calls to two lookouts in the crow's nest high above him. *(Cut to . . .)*   1110 / LS **B32** *45*

(From below) The sailor at the rangefinder slowly turns it clockwise to scan the horizon. *(Cut to . . .)*   1111 / MS **B33** *54*

(From beneath) A long, shining cannon barrel silhouetted against the sky stretches diagonally down across the screen. Black smoke races by in the sky behind it. A sailor steps up to the barrel and stares offscreen. *(Cut to . . .)*   1112 / MS **B34** *53*

The sailor at the rangefinder continues to swing his instrument through its arc. *(Cut to . . .)*   1113 / CU **B35** *92*

1112

(From below) The two lookouts in the crow's nest talk to their shipmate at his post just under them. *(Cut to . . .)*	1114 / **B36**	LS 38
(From below) The sailor at the rangefinder now swings it slowly in the reverse direction. *(Cut to . . .)*	1115 / **B37**	CU 54
A vast stretch of open sea fills the screen. Far off, three very small black shapes break the horizon line. *(Cut to . . .)*	1116 / **F1**	LS 51
(From below) The sailor at the rangefinder leaps from his instrument and bellows a warning to those on deck. *(Cut to . . .)*	1117 / **G1**	CU 21
"Enemy sighted!" *(Cut to . . .)*	TITLE	69
(From beneath) The sailor with his hand on the big cannon turns to peer up at the lookout. He calls urgently, waving his arm. *(Cut to . . .)*	1118 / **G2**	MS 20
(From below) The lookout at the rangefinder station hurries back to his instrument. *(Cut to . . .)*	1119 / **G3**	LS 26
From beneath) The sailor at the cannon turns abruptly and leaps down, out of the frame. Beyond, smoke continues to stream past in the sky. *(Cut to . . .)*	1120 / **G4**	MS 25

1116

1117

(From beneath) Crewmen run over an open grille in the deck above the camera. *(Cut to . . .)*	1121 / MS **G5** 45
Below deck, Matyushenko hurries down a stairway and leans through a doorway to shout the news. *(Cut to . . .)*	1122 / MS **D13** 62
The sailor in the folding chair is startled to wakefulness by the cry. *(Cut to . . .)*	1123 / ECU **G6** 26
The dark-jacketed sailor whirls around on the couch and stares up with alert eyes. *(Cut to . . .)*	1124 / CU **G7** 15
The sailor in the folding chair begins to rise. *(Cut to . . .)*	1125 / ECU **G8** 5
The dark-jacketed sailor springs to his feet. *(Cut to . . .)*	1126 / ECU **G9** 20
The sailor sleeping with knees drawn up under a blanket wakes with a start and struggles to a sitting position. *(Cut to . . .)*	1127 / CU **G10** 31
The two sailors in the officers' lounge leap to their feet, reach for their hats and rush out. *(Cut to . . .)*	1128 / MS **G11** 36
The third sailor whips the blanket off his knees and lunges from his couch toward the door. *(Cut to . . .)*	1129 / CU **G12** 32

(From below) Sailors rush by on the open grille flooring of the deck above a small enclosed area. *(Cut to . . .)* — 1130 / MS — **G13** — *30*

Below deck, Matyushenko stands with his back to the camera looking down a dark stairway. He steps back as a young sailor hurries up the stairs. Matyushenko tells him to go quickly to his post above. As the sailor leaves, another appears at the head of the gangway. *(Cut to . . .)* — 1131 / CU — **D14** — *74*

Two sailors race up a stairway behind Matyushenko. As the dark-jacketed sailor moves into view, Matyushenko grasps his arm and detains him. *(Cut to . . .)* — 1132 / CU — **D15** — *54*

Matyushenko, his back to the camera, opens wide the sailor's dark jacket, exposing a striped seaman's shirt underneath. *(Cut to . . .)* — 1133 / CU — **D16** — *25*

The sailor starts to take off his dark jacket. *(Cut to . . .)* — 1134 / CU — **D17** — *33*

On deck, three sailors start climbing up two huge davits that support one of the *Potemkin*'s lifeboats. *(Cut to . . .)* — 1135 / LS — **G14** — *65*

Matyushenko places a white sailor's cap on his shipmate's head. *(Cut to . . .)* — 1136 / CU — **D18** — *66*

Matyushenko gives the sailor a friendly shove up the stairway leading to the deck and follows him with quick steps. *(Cut to . . .)* — 1137 / CU — **D19** — *39*

Two sailors, above deck, climb the great arch of a lifeboat davit, staring out to sea toward the approaching vessels. *(Cut to . . .)* — 1138 / MS — **G15** — *83*

Four sailors below deck mount a stairway leading upward. *(Cut to . . .)* — 1139 / CU — **G16** — *38*

Two sailors climb rapidly up a narrow ladder attached to the side of a huge funnel. As the first sailor moves up out of the frame, the second sailor enters the frame from below and follows him upward quickly. *(Cut to . . .)* — 1140 / MS — **G17** — *56*

The first sailor climbs to a small lookout platform near the top of the funnel. The second sailor climbs up beside him. — 1141 / MS — **G18** — *71*

They both peer toward the horizon. *(Cut to . . .)*

Across the empty sea that fills the screen, three ships are barely visible on the far horizon. *(Cut to . . .)*

1142 / LS
F2   56

Both sailors on the funnel see the approaching squadron and point excitedly toward the horizon. *(Cut to . . .)*

1143 / MS
G19   27

(From below) The lookout manning the rangefinder swings his instrument to get a fix on the Czarist ships. *(Cut to . . .)*

1144 / MS
G20   45

Silhouetted against the sky, three sailors cling to perches on the arching lifeboat davits as they search for the oncoming squadron. *(Cut to . . .)*

1145 / LS
G21   34

A third sailor joins the two lookouts on a lifeboat davit, straining to catch sight of the enemy. *(Cut to . . .)*

1146 / MS
G22   45

One after the other, four more sailors enter the frame from below as they climb up the narrow iron ladder on the funnel. *(Cut to . . .)*

1147 / MS
G23   96

Ten sailors cling to the small lookout platform near the top of the funnel, all peering offscreen toward the opposing ships of the Czarist navy. *(Cut to . . .)*

1148 / MS
G24   38

1140

Matyushenko holds the small curving boatswain's pipe to his lips and swings his head from left to right as he blows. *(Cut to . . .)*	1149 / ECU **D20** *10*
All hands on deck! *(Cut to . . .)*	TITLE *81*
A bugler, moving to the left, sounds the alarm. *(Cut to . . .)*	1150 / CU **H1** *5*
The bugler, now facing toward the right, continues to blow the alarm. *(Cut to . . .)*	1151 / ECU **H2** *10*
On deck, a boatswain pipes the warning as he pivots to be heard in all quarters. *(Cut to . . .)*	1152 / CU **H3** *25*
At a corner of the deck, a door swings wide. Three sailors emerge and scatter in different directions. *(Cut to . . .)*	1153 / MS **H4** *61*
"To battle stations!" *(Cut to . . .)*	TITLE *85*
The bugler begins to turn toward the camera. *(Cut to . . .)*	1154 / CU **H5** *6*
The bugler, his back to the camera, takes a step forward and then pivots around as he blows. *(Cut to . . .)*	1155 / MS **H6** *35*
Elsewhere on deck, a bulkhead swings wide. Five sailors	1156 / MS

1158

follow each other out, hurrying toward various stations. A sixth sailor begins to emerge from the doorway. *(Cut to . . .)* **H7** *64*

Three sailors run past a maze of pipes on deck, each racing toward a different post. *(Cut to . . .)* 1157 / MS **H8** *32*

Blowing his bugle on a stretch of empty deck near a gun battery, the bugler starts to run away from the camera. As he runs, a large number of sailors hurry into the scene from all directions. Some man the guns, whipping off their canvas covers. Others carry ammunition boxes. *(Cut to . . .)* 1158 / MS **H9** *118*

(From overhead) The breech and controls of a small cannon fill the screen. A sailor hurries around the gun toward the firing seat. *(Cut to . . .)* 1159 / CU **H10** *25*

(From overhead) The sailor moves swiftly to take his position on the firing seat. *(Cut to . . .)* 1160 / ECU **H11** *10*

(From overhead) The sailor's hand enters the frame to grasp the elevation wheel on the cannon breech and his foot steps on an iron brace. *(Cut to . . .)* 1161 / ECU **H12** *27*

1165

1169

(From above) The sailor peers through the cannon's range-finder as he clutches the elevation wheel. *(Cut to . . .)*	1162 / CU **H13** 25
Sailors dart out of a passageway on the deck as others run toward it. *(Cut to . . .)*	1163 / MS **H14** 41
Matyushenko removes the boatswain's pipe from his lips and barks an order. *(Cut to . . .)*	1164 / ECU **D21** 12
Running sailors form a wild scramble of bodies and legs as they dash past a corner of the deck in opposite directions. *(Cut to . . .)*	1165 / MS **H15** 63
Two sailors rush into the dim engineroom of the *Potemkin* to man their posts. *(Cut to . . .)*	1166 / MS **C12** 25
A seaman runs along a passageway between huge pistons in the dark engineroom. *(Cut to . . .)*	1167 / MS **C13** 29
Two seamen hurry in the engineroom toward the camera. *(Cut to . . .)*	1168 / MS **C14** 33
On the bridge, Matyushenko takes a voice tube from the seaman on duty, directs him to carry out an assignment and speaks urgently into the mouthpiece. *(Cut to . . .)*	1169 / CU **D22** 73
In the dim engineroom, a seaman hurries to the voice tube	1170 / CU

1170

hanging on a girder. He lifts it off its cradle and listens as another seaman approaches. *(Cut to . . .)*

C15 *81*

At the bridge, Matyushenko issues instructions to the engineroom. *(Cut to . . .)*

1171 / CU
D23 *21*

In the engineroom, the seaman holding the voice tube repeats Matyushenko's commands to two shipmates who begin rapidly turning large iron wheels. *(Cut to . . .)*

1172 / CU
C16 *53*

On deck, a group of sailors runs past an open corridor. *(Cut to . . .)*

1173 / MS
H16 *20*

In a gun turret, two sailors await a rising hoist that carries two cannon shells. *(Cut to . . .)*

1174 / CU
H17 *37*

One after the other, four seamen hasten past the camera, each pushing four shells suspended from a track overhead. *(Cut to . . .)*

1175 / MS
H18 *79*

Three sailors hustle by the camera in the opposite direction, pushing their suspended artillery shells along the overhead track. *(Cut to . . .)*

1176 / CU
H19 *51*

On deck, gun crews bustle about their guns, preparing them for action. *(Cut to . . .)*

1177 / LS
H20 *82*

In the engineroom, the seaman listening to Matyushenko's

1178 / CU

1175

commands from the bridge repeats his instructions to the engine crew. *(Cut to . . .)*	**C17**	*41*
An engineer works the handle of the engineroom telegraph, confirming the orders coming from the bridge above. *(Cut to . . .)*	1179 / CU **C18**	*47*
A seaman's hand replaces the voice tube on its cradle and picks up another next to it. *(Cut to . . .)*	1180 / ECU **C19**	*54*
Three seamen hurry down the ship's embarkation ladder, which reaches to the water's edge. One of them removes the rails from the lower landing platform, and they start back. *(Cut to . . .)*	1181 / LS **H21**	*95*
In the engineroom, the engineer swings the engineroom telegraph handle from side to side, confirming the orders given him. *(Cut to . . .)*	1182 / CU **C20**	*26*
At the water's edge, the embarkation ladder begins to rise out of the frame. *(Cut to . . .)*	1183 / LS **H22**	*16*
The embarkation ladder slowly rises to a horizontal position above the waves. *(Cut to . . .)*	1184 / MS **H23**	*63*
A sailor begins to stow the upper landing platform of the embarkation ladder, lashing it in preparation for the coming	1185 / CU **H24**	*33*

battle. A pulley is attached to the platform. *(Cut to . . .)*

In the engineroom, a seaman adjusts a control handle above his head. *(Cut to . . .)*	1186 / ECU **C21**	19
On deck, a seaman's hand releases its grip on the pulley attached to the upper landing platform. The platform begins to fold upward against the deck. *(Cut to . . .)*	1187 / CU **H25**	41
Suspended by pulleys above the waves, the entire embarkation ladder slowly twists upward as it is stowed away. *(Cut to . . .)*	1188 / LS **H26**	36
The embarkation ladder rises diagonally across the screen. Behind it the morning sea glitters in the sun. *(Cut to . . .)*	1189 / CU **H27**	24
The embarkation ladder, now hanging at right angles to the deck, swings slowly on its cables. *(Cut to . . .)*	1190 / LS **H28**	22
A white tarpaulin lies folded on the deck. It is raised by offscreen hands, unfolded and spread flat. A seaman's legs	1191 / CU **H29**	49

walk over it. *(Cut to . . .)*

Four seamen on deck hurry to a cluster of artillery shells 1192 / CU
suspended from an overhead track. Each lifts off a shell and **H30** 44
moves out of the frame. *(Cut to . . .)*

Seamen's legs cross over the open tarpaulin spread on deck. 1193 / CU
Shells are placed side by side along one edge of the canvas. **H31** 75
The legs hasten out of the frame. *(Cut to . . .)*

A sailor guides one of the powder charges suspended from 1194 / CU
the ammunition track toward his gun. Another seaman runs **H32** 22
past the camera. *(Cut to . . .)*

A seaman crosses the tarpaulin and lays down the powder 1195 / CU
charge. Other sailors deposit charges and rush away. *(Cut* **H33** 53
to . . .)

A group of seamen dart to the ammunition track, lift off the 1196 / CU
remaining powder charges and turn toward their gun. *(Cut* **H34** 35
to . . .)

On the bridge, Matyushenko pushes his way past a seaman, 1197 / CU

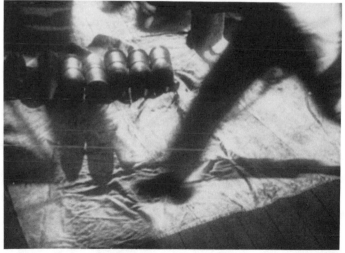

1193

1202

calls urgently into the voice tube, then turns back to his post. **D24** *70*
(Cut to . . .)

Full Speed Ahead *(Cut to . . .)* TITLE *84*

In the engineroom, the chief engineer, with voice tube to his   1198 / CU
ear, issues quick instructions to the seamen on either side of   **C22**   *58*

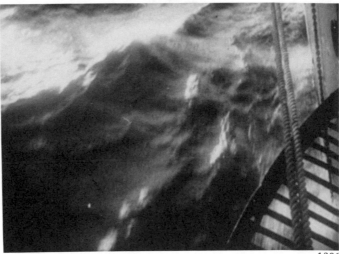

1206

him. They turn handles rapidly and adjust control knobs. *(Cut to . . .)*

On the bridge, Matyushenko speaks urgently into a tube as the seaman at the helm moves the wheel a few degrees. *(Cut to . . .)*
1199 / CU
D25   *35*

Two large pistons, shining with grease, move quickly up and down as the ship's speed increases. *(Cut to . . .)*
1200 / CU
C23   *73*

A great piston head slides up and down with a powerful plunging motion. *(Cut to . . .)*
1201 / ECU
C24   *27*

Two enormous trails of black smoke stream across the screen from the *Potemkin*'s funnels. *(Cut to . . .)*
1202 / LS
I 1   *46*

In the engineroom, a seaman tends an enormous piston as it flashes rapidly up and down. *(Cut to . . .)*
1203 / CU
C25   *86*

A large camshaft in the engineroom rotates so swiftly its circular flight is blurred. *(Cut to . . .)*
1204 / CU
C26   *49*

Under a bright beam of light, the rotating engine shaft whirls with blinding speed. *(Cut to . . .)*
1205 / CU
C27   *39*

(From above) Churning waves surge past the *Potemkin*'s port side. *(Cut to . . .)*
1206 / MS
I 2   *57*

The broad wake of the battleship streams away to the rear. *(Cut to . . .)*
1207 / LS
I 3   *62*

(From above) In the foreground, the lashed embarkation ladder hangs over the water. Beyond, mottled, foaming waves sweep by the ship's starboard side. *(Cut to . . .)*
1208 / LS
I 4   *64*

Two giant pistons in the engineroom move powerfully in short, swift arcs as they propel the *Potemkin* at high speed. *(Cut to . . .)*
1209 / CU
C28   *40*

A whirling, gleaming off-center engine shaft rotates rhythmically. *(Cut to . . .)*
1210 / CU
C29   *47*

The square end of a plunging steam-engine piston darts up and down in a shining blur. *(Cut to . . .)*
1211 / ECU
C30   *38*

(From above) Glittering waves foam past the port side of the
1212 / MS

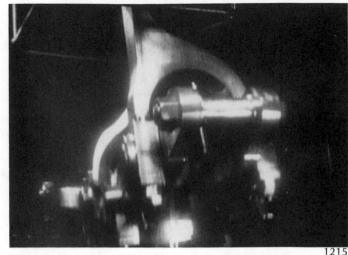

ship. *(Cut to . . .)*	**I 5**	*31*
The sides of two rotating engine pistons whirl past each other like moons in orbit. *(Cut to . . .)*	1213 / CU **C31**	*37*
The faces of two rotating engine pistons spin around each other. *(Cut to . . .)*	1214 / CU **C32**	*29*
The end of a plunging piston rocks with violent energy as it moves in tempo with the ship's furious forward drive. *(Cut to . . .)*	1215 / CU **C33**	*53*
Two enormous trails of black smoke from the *Potemkin*'s funnels stream across the screen. *(Cut to . . .)*	1216 / LS **I 6**	*40*
Across the wide, glistening sea the battleship's turbulent smoke trail drifts backward, darkening the waves beneath. *(Cut to . . .)*	1217 / LS **I 7**	*103*
On the bridge, Matyushenko puts down the voice tube to listen to a seaman's message. *(Cut to . . .)*	1218 / CU **D26**	*48*
(From below) Silhouetted against the sky, two of the *Potemkin*'s port cannon swing slowly in unison toward their target. *(Cut to . . .)*	1219 / LS **J1**	*62*
(From above) The hands of the seaman operating the cannon carefully turn the iron wheel which controls the can-	1220 / CU **H35**	*31*

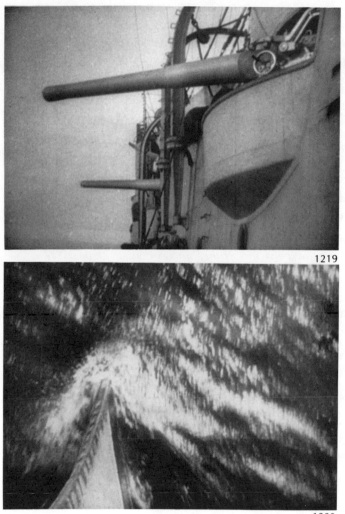

1219

1223

non's aim. *(Cut to . . .)*

(From below) The two port cannon continue their slow swing toward their target. *(Cut to . . .)*	1221 / **J2**	LS 30
The seaman seated at the firing controls of the port cannon adjusts his weapon's position. *(Cut to . . .)*	1222 / **H36**	MS 32
Top Speed *(Cut to . . .)*	TITLE	84

(From directly overhead) The *Potemkin's* knifelike prow cuts sharply through the waters streaming downward across the screen. *(Cut to . . .)*	1223 / MS I 8 47
(From above) The heaving waves surge by the port side of the ship. *(Cut to . . .)*	1224 / MS I 9 47
(From above) Foaming, broken waves shoot past the starboard side under the raised embarkation ladder. *(Cut to . . .)*	1225 / LS I 10 53
White-capped waves churn and break as they rush diagonally across the screen from top to bottom. *(Cut to . . .)*	1226 / CU I 11 41
On the bridge, Matyushenko peers out over the ocean while the helmsman keeps the *Potemkin* on course. *(Cut to . . .)*	1227 / CU D27 16
Matyushenko, his hands empty, turns to the rack behind him and reaches for a spyglass. He faces forward and begins to raise the glass to his eye. *(Cut to . . .)*	1228 / CU D28 25
Far across the ocean, the Czarist squadron approaches steadily under a long, dark trail of smoke. *(Cut to . . .)*	1229 / LS F3 32
Matyushenko puts down his glass and points to the engine-room telegraph in front of the helmsman. *(Cut to . . .)*	1230 / CU D29 33
On the engineroom telegraph, the inner indicator and the outer lever are moved to new positions. *(Cut to . . .)*	1231 / ECU D30 51
In the engineroom, the chief engineer listens at the voice tube as a seaman rapidly turns a valve handle. *(Cut to . . .)*	1232 / CU C34 38
The inner and outer indicators on the engineroom telegraph swing to new positions as the helmsman carries out Matyushenko's orders. *(Cut to . . .)*	1233 / ECU D31 43
(From above) At the breech of a cannon on deck the range-finder operator turns one of his instruments as he adjusts the aim. *(Cut to . . .)*	1234 / CU H37 42
In the distance, the battleships gathering to smash the	1235 / LS

mutiny begin to form a ring around the *Potemkin*. *(Cut to . . .)*	**F4**	*58*

In the engineroom of the *Potemkin,* the shining pistons plunge frantically up and down as they drive the battleship toward its destiny. *(Cut to . . .)* — 1236 / ECU **C35** *34*

(From above) The sailor at the cannon's rangefinder slowly adjusts his elevation and deflection. *(Cut to . . .)* — 1237 / CU **H38** *28*

The cannoneer continues to adjust his weapon's elevation. *(Cut to . . .)* — 1238 / MS **H39** *28*

(From above) The hands of the cannoneer keep moving the wheel as he seeks the range of the oncoming battleships. *(Cut to . . .)* — 1239 / ECU **H40** *26*

In the dark of the engineroom, the pistons flash up and down. *(Cut to . . .)* — 1240 / ECU **C36** *7*

The spinning shaft of the engine moves two giant arms in — 1241 / ECU

staccato rhythm. *(Cut to . . .)*	**C37**	*26*
The inner hand of the engineroom telegraph moves to another position. *(Cut to . . .)*	1242 / ECU **D32**	*30*
The *Potemkin*'s moving pistons flash in the gloom of the engineroom. *(Cut to . . .)*	1243 / ECU **C38**	*25*
(From above) White-capped waves churn past under a lashed boom on the port side of the speeding ship. *(Cut to . . .)*	1244 / MS **I 12**	*56*
(From above) The speeding waves fly diagonally across the screen beyond a lashed steel ladder on the port side. *(Cut to . . .)*	1245 / MS **I 13**	*30*
(From below) Heavy black smoke pours from the *Potemkin*'s funnel, flowing diagonally across the screen. *(Cut to . . .)*	1246 / LS **I 14**	*32*
On the bridge, Matyushenko directs the helmsman as he rapidly turns his helm. *(Cut to . . .)*	1247 / CU **D33**	*26*
Across the open sea, six ships of the gathering enemy squadron form an ever tighter ring around the speeding *Potemkin*. *(Cut to . . .)*	1248 / LS **F5**	*62*

1249

The Potemkin and Torpedo Boat 267 *(Cut to . . .)*	TITLE	*102*

(Aerial view) Far below, the *Potemkin* and its small accompanying torpedo boat cut white grooves across the open sea as they speed to breach the wall of enemy ships. *(Cut to . . .)* — 1249 / LS **I 15** *35*

On the *Potemkin*'s bridge, Matyushenko peers grimly toward the squadron. *(Cut to . . .)* — 1250 / CU **D34** *41*

The flagship is advancing! *(Cut to . . .)* — TITLE *93*

Closing in behind the *Potemkin,* the opposing squadron gains on the mutinying sailors and their vessel. *(Cut to . . .)* — 1251 / LS **F6** *49*

(From below) The funnel of the *Potemkin* belches black smoke across the screen. *(Cut to . . .)* — 1252 / LS **I 16** *29*

The ocean, churned white by the speeding *Potemkin,* slips swiftly past under a boom lashed on the port side. *(Cut to . . .)* — 1253 / MS **I 17** *44*

The waves continue to flow by the battleship's port side under a lashed steel ladder. *(Cut to . . .)* — 1254 / MS **I 18** *36*

On the bridge, Matyushenko replaces his spyglass on the rack behind him and observes the helmsman as he turns his — 1255 / CU **D35** *50*

1258

1259

wheel. *(Cut to . . .)*

(From below) On the port side, the *Potemkin's* armored   1256 / MS
cannon swings slowly in a wide arc. *(Cut to . . .)*   J3   85

The squadron is nearing us! *(Cut to . . .)*   TITLE   92

Across the open sea, nearer than ever, the gathering enemy   1257 / LS

squadron now steams within direct firing range. *(Cut to . . .)*	**F7**	*58*
Less than a thousand yards away, two huge battleships of the pursuing fleet bear down at full steam on the *Potemkin.* *(Cut to . . .)*	1258 / LS **F8**	*45*
(From above) The hands of the crewman aiming the *Potemkin*'s port-side cannon slowly turn a wheel to keep the oncoming ships in line of fire. *(Cut to . . .)*	1259 / ECU **H41**	*25*
(From below) The shadow of a moving cannon barrel creeps across the *Potemkin*'s hull. *(Cut to . . .)*	1260 / MS **J4**	*29*
(From below) The armored turret of the ship's port cannon swings slowly across the screen. *(Cut to . . .)*	1261 / MS **J5**	*31*
Inside the armored turret, the gun crew hurriedly removes a shell from its overhead carrier. *(Cut to . . .)*	1262 / MS **H42**	*43*
The gun crew rushes the shell to the cannon. *(Cut to . . .)*	1263 / MS **H43**	*13*
(From below) Black smoke from the *Potemkin*'s funnel drifts backward past a cannon barrel. *(Cut to . . .)*	1264 / LS **I 19**	*70*
Glittering, white-capped waves sweep across the screen. *(Cut to . . .)*	1265 / CU **I 20**	*37*
(From below) Black smoke continues to drift backward past the barrel of the *Potemkin*'s main gun. *(Cut to . . .)*	1266 / LS **I 21**	*48*
Huge plumes of thick smoke pour from the *Potemkin*'s two funnels and stream across the screen. *(Cut to . . .)*	1267 / LS **I 22**	*37*
A long plume of black smoke drifts across the empty sky, darkening the shining waters beneath it. *(Cut to . . .)*	1268 / LS **I 23**	*89*
On the bridge, Matyushenko stares tensely toward the squadron. *(Cut to . . .)*	1269 / CU **D36**	*28*
Two huge battleships of the Czarist fleet bear down on the *Potemkin,* their prows submerged in flying spray. *(Cut to . . .)*	1270 / LS **F9**	*50*

On the bridge, Matyushenko leans forward suddenly to operate a signal. *(Cut to . . .)* 1271 / CU **D37**   *18*

Matyushenko's hand picks up the voice tube from its hook and lifts it out of the frame. *(Cut to . . .)* 1272 / CU **D38**   *21*

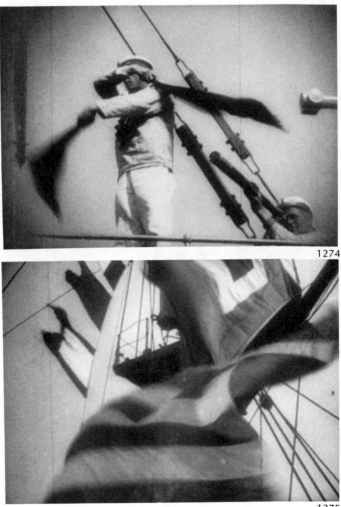

1274

1275

"Run up the signal: Don't fight—join us!" *(Cut to . . .)* TITLE *145*

Matyushenko's hand reenters the frame to replace the voice tube on its hook. *(Cut to . . .)* 1273 / CU
D39 *25*

(From below) Silhouetted against the sky, a sailor with a semaphore flag in each hand sends the *Potemkin*'s plea to the oncoming squadron. *(Cut to . . .)* 1274 / MS
K1 *68*

Join . . . *(Cut to . . .)* TITLE *66*

(From below) The wind-whipped signal flags of the battleship stretch along a halyard from deck to crow's nest with their brotherly plea. *(Cut to . . .)* 1275 / MS
K2 *44*

. . . us! *(Cut to . . .)* TITLE *66*

Four groups of signal flags rise slowly on their halyards toward the yardarm high above the deck. *(Cut to . . .)* 1276 / LS
K3 *32*

(From below) A line of flags slowly rises across the screen in front of the crow's nest. *(Cut to . . .)* 1277 / LS
K4 *15*

The four groups of signal flags continue upward past the yardarm. *(Cut to . . .)* 1278 / LS
K5 *17*

The ocean, churned white by the speeding *Potemkin,* slips by under a lashed boom on the port side. *(Cut to . . .)* 1279 / MS
I 24 *33*

The waves continue to rush by under a lashed steel ladder on the port side. *(Cut to . . .)* 1280 / MS
I 25 *42*

The tumbling waves sweep diagonally across the screen. *(Cut to . . .)* 1281 / CU
I 26 *29*

(From below) A giant billow of dark smoke from the *Potemkin*'s funnel sweeps past the control tower and across the screen. *(Cut to . . .)* 1282 / LS
I 27 *37*

The turbulent jet of smoke from the forward funnel flows rearward over the ship. *(Cut to . . .)* 1283 / LS
I 28 *30*

(From below) The *Potemkin*'s giant main cannon, silhouetted against the sky, stretches diagonally across the screen. Behind it, the flying smoke races across the screen in the 1284 / MS
J6 *39*

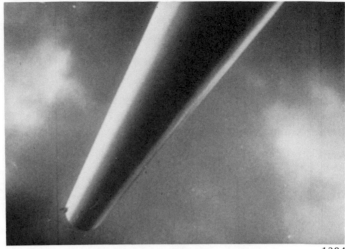

1284

same direction. *(Cut to . . .)*

Inside the gun turret the sailor aiming the cannon rapidly whirls a small wheel as he presses his eye to the rangefinder. *(Cut to . . .)*	1285 / CU **H44** *21*

Inside the gun turret the sailor aiming the cannon rapidly whirls a small wheel as he presses his eye to the rangefinder. *(Cut to . . .)*   1285 / CU   **H44**   *21*

In the dark gun turret, a seaman stands at the open breech of the cannon. He turns and speaks rapidly to two sailors. *(Cut to . . .)*   1286 / MS   **H45**   *28*

The enemy is within range. *(Cut to . . .)*   TITLE   *93*

In the turret, the seaman peering through the rangefinder holds the aiming wheel steady. His weapon is "on target" and ready to fire. *(Cut to . . .)*   1287 / CU   **H46**   *55*

A mustached seaman in the turret stares outward, waiting to spring to action. *(Cut to . . .)*   1288 / CU   **H47**   *28*

The seamen at the cannon's open breech and his two ship-mates stand tense and motionless. *(Cut to . . .)*   1289 / MS   **H48**   *38*

A huge cannon shell in the hands of a waiting sailor gleams dully in the dim light of the *Potemkin*'s gun turret. *(Cut to . . .)*   1290 / ECU   **H49**   *37*

Four crewmen stand in the turret, immobile, in a breathless wait for the signal to fire. *(Cut to . . .)*   1291 / MS   **H50**   *23*

All for one. *(Cut to . . .)* TITLE 76

The massive main gun turret of the *Potemkin* swings in a grim arc that faces its three black cannon muzzles directly at the camera. *(Cut to . . .)* 1292 / LS
J7   168

(From above) Two of the *Potemkin*'s gun barrels point directly astern. *(Cut to . . .)* 1293 / CU
J8   38

Like giant primeval beasts, the three main guns of the battleship rise slowly one after the other to point at the sky. *(Cut to . . .)* 1294 / LS
J9   187

Against an empty sky the crow's nest is seen high in the distance. After a moment, the huge black muzzle of a giant cannon rises into view in the immediate foreground, a mailed fist prepared to strike. *(Cut to . . .)* 1295 / CU
J10   96

1291

One for all. *(Cut to . . .)* TITLE *100*

(From below) At the top of the *Potemkin*'s highest mast the 1296 / LS
mutineers' banner whips staunchly in the fresh breeze. *(Cut* **K6** *30*
to . . .)

(From below) The muzzle of a mammoth cannon rises into 1297 / CU

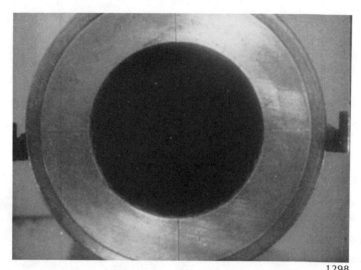

1298

view, filling the entire screen. *(Cut to . . .)* **J11** *30*

The black opening of the cannon muzzle stares pointblank 1298 / ECU
into the camera. *(Cut to . . .)* **J12** *23*

On the bridge, Matyushenko peers tensely out toward the 1299 / CU
oncoming squadron. He issues terse instructions to the **D40** *29*
helmsman. *(Cut to . . .)*

Breathing vast clouds of smoke, two pursuing battleships of 1300 / LS
the Czarist squadron loom ever larger as they close in. *(Cut* **F10** *60*
to . . .)

Inside the *Potemkin*'s gun turret, two of the seamen shake 1301 / MS
hands and kiss in a brotherly embrace before the expected **H51** *36*
holocaust begins. *(Cut to . . .)*

The *Potemkin*'s middle cannon muzzle rises slowly from beneath the frame until its deadly black circle fills the entire screen in head-on confrontation. *(Cut to . . .)*

1302 / ECU
J13   76

The two seamen in the turret end their farewell embrace and step back to their posts at the giant gun. *(Cut to . . .)*

1303 / MS
H52   17

The huge black aperture of the cannon muzzle fills the screen head-on. *(Cut to . . .)*

1304 / ECU
J14   26

On the bridge, Matyushenko anxiously rubs his chin in an agony of suspense. *(Cut to . . .)*

1305 / CU
D41   28

Two of the *Potemkin*'s cannon point directly at the camera. Behind and above them the ship's control tower rises in tiers like an armored carapace. Not a sailor is seen. The entire ship seems to be holding its breath. *(Cut to . . .)*

1306 / LS
J15   18

1301

(From above) Two barrels of the *Potemkin*'s forward guns aim straight along the empty deck, ominously waiting. *(Cut to . . .)*	1307 / MS J16 *31*
The dark opening of a cannon's muzzle fills the screen head-on . . . waiting. *(Cut to . . .)*	1308 / ECU J17 *15*
Will they fire . . . *(Cut to . . .)*	TITLE *77*
A seaman in the turret stares out tensely. *(Cut to . . .)*	1309 / CU H53 *24*
A sailor's anxiously drawn brows and squinting eyes fill the screen. *(Cut to . . .)*	1310 / ECU H54 *18*
A seaman's hand clutches a hanging cannon lanyard in readiness for the command that will send the *Potemkin*'s first shell on its way. *(Cut to . . .)*	1311 / ECU H55 *18*
The black circle of the point-blank muzzle filling the screen moves slightly downward. *(Cut to . . .)*	1312 / ECU J18 *24*
. . . or . . . *(Cut to . . .)*	TITLE *62*
In the turret, a seaman waits, tensely poised as he stares offscreen. *(Cut to . . .)*	1313 / CU H56 *22*
In the engineroom, the pistons race madly like a powerfully beating heart driving the great ship. *(Cut to . . .)*	1314 / ECU C39 *25*
The prow of the speeding *Potemkin* seen almost head-on veers across the screen in a new direction. *(Cut to . . .)*	1315 / LS I 29 *43*
In the turret, two seamen stand immobile with a shell and powder charge in their arms. *(Cut to . . .)*	1316 / CU H57 *22*
On the turret floor, six shells and eight powder charges lie waiting their turn to fly to their targets. *(Cut to . . .)*	1317 / CU H58 *22*
In the turret, two seamen wait at their gun posts while the loaders grip the shells in their arms. *(Cut to . . .)*	1318 / MS H59 *25*
The intent faces of three *Potemkin* crewmen fill the screen. Suddenly, on one of the faces the eyebrows raise, the tense	1319 / ECU L1 *38*

1319

mouth eases and a jubilant expression begins to dawn. *(Cut to . . .)*

Brothers! *(Cut to . . .)*	TITLE	*98*

The face of a cheering, elated sailor fills the screen. His arm stretches high out of the frame. *(Cut to . . .)* — 1320 / ECU **L2** *3*

Another sailor's exultant face fills the screen. Behind it, a seaman's white arm is raised high. *(Cut to . . .)* — 1321 / ECU **L3** *6*

(From above) Sailors race out from the *Potemkin*'s interior and swarm across the entire forward quarterdeck of the battleship. *(Cut to . . .)* — 1322 / LS **L4** *34*

(From below) Seamen running over a barred deck area are seen from a lower level. *(Cut to . . .)* — 1323 / CU **L5** *31*

The shouting, cheering face of a third sailor fills the screen. *(Cut to . . .)* — 1324 / ECU **L6** *16*

(From below) The banner of the *Potemkin*'s mutineers whips briskly on the topmost mast. *(Cut to . . .)*	1325 / LS	
	K7	*35*
The *Potemkin's* three stern cannon slowly lower to deck level. *(Cut to . . .)*	1326 / LS	
	J19	*54*
(From below) The starboard deck rails stand vacant. Suddenly they are thronged with cheering, cap-waving sailors. *(Cut to . . .)*	1327 / LS	
	L7	*41*
(From below) Crewmen quickly jam the deck rails and swing their caps excitedly. *(Cut to . . .)*	1328 / LS	
	L8	*45*
In the foreground, two *Potemkin* crewmen wave their caps fraternally at a Czarist cruiser which has approached to within a thousand yards. The cruiser's rails are crowded with friendly sailors. *(Cut to . . .)*	1329 / LS	
	F11	*66*
The camera glides past the thronged forward deck of the *Potemkin* and circles around its great prow. Every open area of the ship is jammed with jubilant, cheering crewmen. *(Cut to . . .)*	1330 / LS	
	L9	*200*
Over the heads of the Czarist admirals roared a brotherly cheer. *(Cut to . . .)*	TITLE	*142*

1329

1332

(From the water line) On deck, the *Potemkin*'s elated sailors begin throwing their caps into the air. *(Cut to . . .)*

1331 / LS
L10 45

(From the water line) White caps fly through the air as the *Potemkin*'s sailors gathered at the rails celebrate their unexpected victory. *(Cut to . . .)*

1332 / LS
L11 32

(From the water line) In another deck area, crewmen fling their caps exuberantly into the air. *(Cut to . . .)*

1333 / LS
L12 27

Cheering, waving seamen line the *Potemkin*'s rails. Behind them, black smoke drifts overhead. *(Cut to . . .)*

1334 / MS
L13 32

Thick smoke swirls across a group of happy sailors massed on the *Potemkin*'s bridge. *(Cut to . . .)*

1335 / MS
L14 47

A Czarist battleship far across the water is partially obscured by great clouds of black smoke. *(Cut to . . .)*

1336 / LS
F12 38

The *Potemkin* sails by, moving out of the frame as its smoke pours back across the waters. *(Cut to . . .)*

1337 / LS
I 30 25

Sailors crowd the bridge and upper decks, waving to the friendly crews on the Czarist ships. *(Cut to . . .)*

1338 / LS
L15   *31*

Far across the water the *Potemkin* steams by, passing unmolested through the cordon of steel. *(Cut to . . .)*

1339 / LS*
L16   *20*

(From below) The crowded crow's nest of the *Potemkin* is silhouetted against the sky. From it sailors and signal flags extend cheerful greetings to the other ships. *(Cut to . . .)*

1340 / LS
L17   *42*

(From below) The exuberant mutineers jam the rail of the *Potemkin* and wave to their fellow seamen. *(Cut to . . .)*

1341 / MS
L18   *31*

(From above) In the foreground, the prow and quarterdeck of the *Potemkin* are cut by the bottom frame line. Beyond it, upside down on the surface of the glittering waves, the

1342 / LS
F13   *89*

*The same shot is used in Part I, Shot 6.

dark shadow of a Czarist battleship glides by. Its rails are crowded with the silhouettes of friendly sailors. *(Cut to . . .)*

(From above) The ocean's marbled, glistening waters swell across the screen from top to bottom. *(Cut to . . .)*   1343 / CU
I 31   *35*

(From above) The upside down shadow of the friendly Czarist battleship skims over the glittering waves in front of the *Potemkin*'s prow. *(Cut to . . .)*   1344 / LS
F14   *49*

(From the waterline) The *Potemkin*'s enormous, knife-sharp prow drives straight toward the camera. Far above, its rails are thronged with sailors jubilantly throwing their hats into the air. As the battleship draws steadily closer, its prow looms up like an iron juggernaut about to crush the viewer beneath it. *(Cut to . . .)*   1345 / LS
I 32   *123*

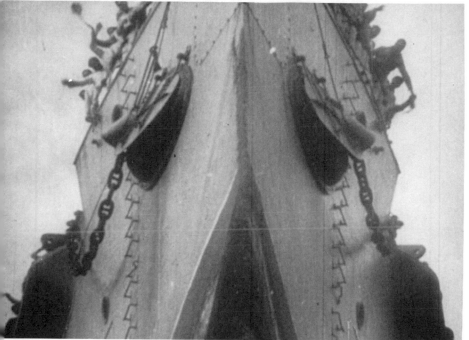

1345

The raw iron prow of the *Potemkin* breaks through the frame with irresistible power. It overruns the screen, carrying its crew to freedom. *(Cut to . . .)*

1346 / ECU
I 33   17

The End.

TITLE   69